AF204319

Imprint:

© 2018 by Arikpo Lawrence Omini

Coverphoto by Armin Linnarz
(License: https://creativecommons.org/licenses/by/4.0/legalcode)

Cover-Design & type setting by
Angelika Fleckenstein; Spotsrock

Printed and published by

tredition GmbH
Halenreie 40-44
22359 Hamburg

ISBN:
978-3-7469-7963-2 (Paperback)
978-3-7469-7964-9 (Hardcover)
978-3-7469-7965-6   (e-Book)

Bibliographic information published by the Deutsche Nationalbibliothek
(German National Library):

The Deutsche Nationalbibliothek (German National Library) has recorded this
publication in the Deutsche Nationalbibliografie (German National Bibliography);
detailed bibliographic data are available through the Internet at http://dnb.d-nb.de.

ARIKPO Lawrence OMINI

GERMANY

HAS
FALLEN

MASS MIGRATION AND **RISE OF POPULISM**
IN THE **EUROPEAN UNION** AND THAT FAMOUS
WALL OF THE **AMERICAN EMPIRE**

ABOUT THE AUTHOR

The Author of this Book, titled; "GERMANY HAS FALLEN" has written a couple of books over a long period. Some of these books were published in the traditional setting in social and cultural circles. Among his recent books are 'WINGS AND WHITE ROBES', a supernatural and historical fantasy thriller novel based around the true nature, life and significance of a mysterious and legendary figure known as the "World Teacher." Also, the novel titled; "LEOPARD KING," a Sci-fi, magic, mythological, action-packed adventure and supernatural fantasy based on the 500 years old historical secret of the Leopard Society of West Africa. In their belief, the Panther King is the King of the skies, jungle, night and King of the Underworld or Afterlife. According to the secret of the Leopard Society, the 'Master of Enlightenment' and 'God of Storm' called 'The World Teacher' will return and would establish his new 'World Kingdom' on earth but for that to be successful he has to wage a successful war against the unseen powerful forces from Astron that bring chaos on earth.

The Author has worked as a columnist and editor of both Trumpet Newspaper and Pathfinder Magazine and has written several articles in several journals and gazettes. He migrated to Germany in 2012. He has spent most of his time studying the population, the political entities, social and working life of many Germans and immigrants in the European Union, and the impact recent migration has had on the country and its institutions and vice versa. He currently lives in Würzburg, a historical city in Bavaria, Southern Germany.

For all correspondence and inquiries, please contact;

Email: arikingomini@outlook.com

DEDICATION

This Book is dedicated to all the tens of thousands of people over the years seeking a better life who have lost their lives while making the perilous journey through the Sahara Desert and the Mediterranean Sea to Europe. In particular, this book is dedicated to Alan Kurdi, the three years old Syrian child refugee who drowned in the Mediterranean Sea in 2015 while making the journey to Europe.

ACKNOWLEDGEMENT

I acknowledge my biological Brothers and Sisters, namely; Peace, William, Essien, Ebri, Ubi, Dorothy, Victoria-Miriam, Magdalene Omini for their support and encouragement towards me. I also acknowledge my friends; Salem Edosomwan, Franziska Cheburashka, Christian Mba and Angelika Flagner among others, for their intelligent and analytical contribution to the writing and finishing of this book.

CONTENT

PROLOGUE

RISE IN ANTI-IMMIGRANTS SENTIMENTS

What is Angela Merkel thinking, letting in all those many migrants and refugees into a fledgling European Union? She masterminded and executed her plan of flooding Europe with foreigners opening up to Muslims and now we're in this political schismatic and discordant climate. She lays out her plan of action, approach and statement of assertion regarding immigration and multi-nationalism, calling on her European counterparts to follow her controversial plan on migration but she has no followers. No one would follow her. Some maintained, they don't believe Germany has become a better place since 2015. Germany has isolated itself with its refugee policy. The population is polarized and becoming radicalized. We have hundreds of thousands of people within the country. We don't know who they are or how they'll turn out … "Merkel Must Go" continued some angry politicians, left- and right-wing groups.

These are some of the publicly declared outrage at the effects of the norm breaking stirring policies, the German Chancellor Angela Merkel was allegedly accused of masterminding and steering to suit her grand action plan on immigration. Although, she tried to keep up the moral ground in the face of criticism from her opposition parties and other right wing political groups, she later made a deal to seal off the route from Turkey across to the European Union with a principle that Germany and Europe can't solve the world's problems by proposing a three billion Euro package to Turkey to support that country control the migration coming from the Middle East.

It's been a wild ride for Europe since then as Hungary had put up a fence to wall out all migrants and asylum seekers coming in through the southern route even proposing a bill that makes helping migrants a crime. Britain has initiated a Brexit plan to leave the European Union due primarily to the issue of migration. There's the radicalization of extreme hate groups such as the Patriotic Europeans Against the Islamization Of the West or 'PEGIDA,' rise in Neo-Nazi and the right-wing populist 'Alternative for Deutschland' party and the emergence of fanatics and opposition within Angela Merkel's coalition government in Germany. Also, the far-right, Freedom Party of Austria with links to the Nazi past that brought the new Chancellor Sebastian Kurz to power. There was also the populist anti-immigrant law and justice party movements in Poland and Italy with the politics of resentment and hate that brought Prime Minister Giuseppe Conte to power as he vowed to tackle the new threat to Europe's stability by promising to deport hundreds of thousands of refugees and asylum seekers out of his country. All of them echoing the same rhetoric of fear, bigotry and intolerance.

This situation reminded me of a German music I heard a night before started writing this book. It kept me awake all night. Not the music melody but its lyrical connection to my emotional state and a conduit it tapped to magnify its electrical effects in my mood causing a whirlwind of a conscious, troubled even confusing thoughts on that night. It told the truth and nothing but the truth stressing that *"Life is a journey that never ends, and no human really knows where he or she is going"*. That journey is what we're going to essentially project in this treatise as it leads many to an uncertain future they call Europe and its many immigration problems.

Recently while attending the 100th Birthday anniversary of Nelson Mandela in South Africa on the 17th July 2018, Barack Obama said *"we are living in strange and uncertain times." "Globalization has increased economic inequality. A few dozen individuals control the amount of wealth as the poorest half of humanity. In many middle incomes and developing countries, new wealth has just tracked the old bad deal that people got because of reinforced or compounded existing inequality. The only difference is, it created even greater op-portunities for corruption on an epic scale.*" Strongmen politics are *ascending suddenly whereby elections in some pretense of democracy are maintained, the form of it, but those in power seek to under-mine every institution or norm that seem to give democracy a mean-ing. Politics of fear, resentment and retrenchment is on the move at a pace unimaginable, a few years ago.* **"Far right parties in the west are on the rise based on the platform of not just protectionism and closed borders but racial nationalism.**" Free press is on the attack. Even social media once seen as a mechanism to promote knowledge, understanding and solidarity, has proved just as effective promoting hatred, paranoia, propaganda and conspiracy theories. *"Should we see that hope as naive and misguided, by the Berlin wall falling?"* "I believe in the vision of equality, justice, freedom, multiracial democ-racy built on the premise that all people are created equal by our Cre-ator with certain inalienable rights." Countries that rely on rabid na-tionalism and xenophobia, doctrines of tribal, racial or religious su-premacy as their main organizing principle are eventually consumed by the same extreme ideology as they descend into wars, even as his-tory has shown us. Populations will be moving, and environmental challenges are not going to go away on their own. "The only way to address problems like mass migration, climate change or pandemic disease will be to develop systems for international cooperation. We are bounded together by our common humanity ..." Continued Obama.

As one presently living thousands of kilometers away in Bavaria, Southern Germany affected by these dangerous outcomes, it was par-ticularly intriguing hearing those words, as they only confirm my fears of uncertainty and dimming prospects of hope. *The 'Berlin Wall' was the symbol of the cold war in the eyes of the west. It rep-resented the ethnic divisions within Germany and the separation of Germany into four different divisive parts governed by the Soviet East and Western world but also as a testament to intolerance, hate,*

bigotry, racism, instability, hopelessness, poverty and sense of inse-
curity not just prevalent in the communist East Germany, Eastern
Europe but also in other parts of the world. Inadvertently, its fall
means the world got to experience a socioeconomic transformation
and a new lease of life away from the painful legacies and negativi-
ties that characterized that old-world order. But over two decades
after the great fall of the wall of apathy, egocentricity, xenophobia,
racial nationalism, inequality, poverty, protectionism, autocratic
control, ethnic and religious divisions, a new illiberal, right wing,
unequal, intolerant, partisan, dogmatic and sexist society nestled in
democratic institutions and a racist mindset is reasserting itself even
as it presents a clear and present danger in today's world.

Recent report states that many Germans are feeling gloomy about the future of their country. While many may be happy with their current financial situation, a turbulent imminent malaise may be on the horizon due to a torrent of issues facing the country. The German economy is booming in 2018, and unemployment is at an all-time low. In spite of the good job prospects, low crime rate and attractive environment, many youths feel problems are seething below the surface. They feel less at ease with the direction the arrow is pointing at. Well, it's easy to fathom why they feel that way. After all, since the summer of 2018, a lot has happened. The country failed to qualify beyond the first round of the World Cup tournament, a situation that hasn't happened for a long time. Mezut Özil, a member of the German national team quit citing racism. In August 2018, a video footage of far-right sympathizers, rioting and chasing foreigners through the streets of Chemnitz, shook the country. Pessimism remains with the rise of the Alternative for Germany (AfD) right wing party. They are worried that what's happening, may be a proof that similar patterns may arise anywhere around the country, in the near future, if the public discourse doesn't change as well as the way people perceive things. But these events, some say, are not isolated or unrelated. The climate change worsens each year damaging crops. Even, the prices of homes and rents, according to Deutsche Bank have risen 80 % in some major cities, while there's a national shortfall of about one million residential units. All this happens as salaries and wages in many public and private establishments doesn't grow at par, with the rate of increase of rents and home prices as some fear, it's only a matter of time before the cost of basic items in the market place rise.

As a foreigner in Germany, affected by these gloomy realities, it places those like me at a disadvantageous position to dream, if those unnerving prospects become real. As the temperature of events around the world rises, and more people coming into the country, the fear is falling in the hands of a bitter immigration officer or judge whose judgment resembles one of those bigots like my former teacher in the German language course who said explicitly, "*Schmeissen sie alle raus*," meaning "Throw them all out". Whose decisions are influenced and fueled by the cry of those on the extreme right whether extreme groups, neo-Nazi or German right-wing political parties who are seeking to further their cause by stoking fear of being invaded or overrun by migrants at their borders. A situation they fear might upset their societal fabric and change their very way of life. Also, a strong reaction to news stories of 2016 January 1st, where it was reported, many in cities such as Cologne and others were sexually assaulted by refugees and migrants in trains and bus stations called "Bahnhof" in Germany. I was left wondering, he knew most, if not all of us in his class were migrants and foreigners but he was unhinged and didn't care if we in that same situation might be affected by such extreme measures. If those in the corridors of power were to heed to his passionate call and implement them, then most migrants and refugees would be caught between a rock and a hard place, a famous German metaphor. But on regular basis we see such laws emerging that limits access to basic civil and legal rights, tending to control and restrict migrants, asylum seekers and refugees as well as the extent of their freedom in that great country or even outright deportation out of Germany.

The disputes over immigration have threatened to divide the European union on several occasions with each country having its own opinion and agenda on how to treat the migration issues in ways that will suit their political goals. There are many refugees and migrants crossing the Mediterranean Sea to reach the frontiers of Europe, so they say. However, in recent times, records show the numbers have drastically reduced. The question is, "what country will take responsibility of them and rightly integrate them into their society?" This toxic issue threatened to bring down Germany's Angela Merkel and alleged to be the cause of the recent rise in Anti immigrants' sentiments in the European Union. Even, Donald Trump was voted to power as President of the United States of America in part because he promised to build the big WALL to keep out migrants and refugees from Mexico and beyond, seeking sanctuary in America. He promoted a bogus concept of America being invaded by radical Muslims, terrorists and drugs from Mexico. "Is it really a migrant crisis or a political one?" Of delusional and idiosyncratic world leaders with false impression who've misinterpreted and contradicted the entire concept of reality and facts, apprehensive on irrational arguments and are confused about their direction while seeking for scapegoats to lay all their blame of incompetence upon? "Do they really care about the many deaths on the sea and the violence and pain undergone by these migrants to reach Europe?" Is the narrative targeting refugees and migrants in Europe and America a digression from the most important issues facing the world right now? Too many things are wrong with the world. "Who'll fix them?" When the same people who should be addressing those global issues including poverty, racial discrimination, injustice, climate change and inequality are bickering about the unfortunate effects of the problem and not the cause. Once again, should we still believe in the change of unification, inclusion, freedom, peace and hope of a brighter future offered the world by the "FALL OF THE BERLIN WALL AND THE SOVIET UNION?" Or should we assume, that in these strange times the invisible BERLIN WALL, THE SOVIET UNION AND A NEW ORWELLIAN AMERICAN EMPIRE has cropped up? I once heard about the story in the 1980s in Berlin, whereby President Ronald Reagan told Russia's President Gorbachev "TEAR DOWN THIS

WALL!" It's an inspiring quote and forms the basis and intrinsic idea behind this book. But if there's anything recent history of mass migration has taught us is that no matter how tall the WALL is, the defiant Migrants, asylum seekers and refugees look taller as they look down on the shrinking WALL unintimidated like a frightened captive who has managed to fight and overcome his monster captor.

What country more in Europe had experienced firsthand accounts of what a war can do to a country but Germany itself. A war that was caused by the forces grounded in the organizing principles of hate, right-wing nationalism, racial superiority, supremacy, anti-Semitism, antipathy, ethnic prejudice and xenophobia. If there was anything the second world war did was that it taught Germany a life changing lesson. The same lesson that probably led to the reconstruction and rapid urban regeneration of the country including social and cultural reforms with higher standards of life and a different way of thinking drawing the power of creativity and unity to bear to actualize its dream of freedom, liberty, prosperity, gender equality and most importantly love and respect for their fellow men and women or I would wish it did. I would like to believe so, if not, how could they have emerged from the ruins of war which Nazi Germany caused that brought torture and pain not withstanding uncountable deaths to innocent victims across Europe but today is the democratic leader of Europe, advocate of social reform and a powerful and economic force to reckon with. Eventually, the 'Giant' still woke up in the end despite stomaching the dark rain of bombs that fell on it like the 'rapture black rain' rupturing and cranking up its fabric blasting towns and blighting out humans, animals and plant life alike. But the "fallen Giant" was up and running again in a few years after the official close of the second world war in 1945. That also reminds me of a film I once watched with a Japanese art of war philosophy that "*a Ninja will always be a Ninja or a Leopard as long it's is not dead when it falls, it'll rise again, maybe stronger than ever before.*" But even in death it might resurrect shedding the old skin like the phoenix rising from the ashes. In this case, positively.

The Germans are strong and resilient in the face of peril but peaceful in the face of a warm economic environment. They have broken down barriers to rise and are still rising, today more than ever, they are a great nation. An economic power nation with a strong integrity index, not just in Europe but around the World. They stand once more, a force not of terror but of good to bring prosperity, justice, peace, order and unity now to a continuously more uncertain, divided, bruised and somewhat fractured European union and the world community. "But who cares if the United Kingdom leaves the Union?" The mighty Germany is there to hold the Union together with its economic muscle and the allure of respect it attracts from other members of the union and beyond. But that also brings us to another topic of conversation of the significance and role the immigrants, migrants and refugees plays in an economy such as that of Europe and Germany in particular. Like one analyst put it, it's something you can't estimate or measure because it runs through out every facet of the system of the government entity felt in the socioeconomic and political nerve of the country.

Who else can gauge such indices as a mathematical indicator with value but the German people and economists themselves unless they want to ignore that fact. Even, the government of Germany back in the fall of 2015, said; the positive effects of a million migrants' entry into Germany in that year in the area of the economy were already beginning to bear fruits. And I can't stop but wonder that perhaps the increasing economic surplus of the country maybe a domino effect of that particular migration that recorded a huge influx of people all at once to live in the new society. Like a friend of mine, said to me *"Behold I saw something, a transient vision as I watched television, on the day of the event of the 'March of Hope' of thousands of Syrians that took place in September 4th 2015 after many fagged out and exhausted refugees who were trapped in-front of the Keleti railway station of Budapest were allowed to come to Germany by the Bundeskanzlerin Angela Merkel. As they walked, they were many illumi-*

*nating **stars** dancing on the faces of many of the beleaguered march-
ing migrants and refugees and a huge **pillar of light** behind them as
they walked on the road to the destination and land of their dreams."*
Germany is that migrant's paradise, their golden land of dreams or
the colossus.

A majority of Germans are faithful people who believe in God.
Even though the statistics of religious services and church attendance
is on the downward spiral. Survey shows China and Europe are both
atheist capital of the world. *"I quite remember in 2016, during the
American Presidential elections, on YouTube were dream testimonies of many people over 80 % surveyed who dreamt that Donald
Trump and not Hillary Clinton would win the General Elections. A
fire man particularly predicted that the stock market and economy
will boom when he wins. Today, all those visions turned out to be
true."* But whether Germans believe it or not, the upward swing in
the curve of the wave of good economic tidings in recent years may
not be deeply unconnected to the entrance of immigrants, migrants
and refugees not just out of Syria but from Africa, Middle East nations, Asia and other European nations, of which active presence and
social well being translates to vibrant entrepreneurial, innovation,
service based economy, strong buying power and value added tax
leading to economic growth. Many migrants arrive with skills and
contribute to human capital development of receiving countries in
Europe. Labour migrants have the most positive impact on the public
purse. Employment is the single biggest determinant of migrants' net
fiscal contribution. Migrants boost the working age population and
contribute to technological progress. The role and significance of migration cannot be overemphasized especially if the host countries
such as Germany, maximize the benefits of it and improve migrants
and refugee's employability situation including true integration. By
true integration, unlike countries such as in Africa, Middle East and
Asia, the receiving countries such as Germany creates a multi national society based on symbiosis as they offer sanctuary and opportunities to the migrants and refugees, while equipping themselves

with a wealth of human resources and information to gather, learn, sensitize, grow and build their collective future projections from.

In conclusion, social and economic integration will mean host country citizens no longer bolstered by ethnocentric values and skepticism will get to meet, interact, understand, adjust to certain changes and support the refugees and migrants to realize not just the contrast in their cultures but the essence of diffusion of other cultures to create a broader trust and empathy rather than suspicion and rejection of outsiders as well as find strength in their pool of diversity. In a similar vein, economic integration, by host countries, don't have to continue in their old ways by which refugees and asylum seekers are settled, as they are placed in hostels separated from the rest of the society. But to ensure regardless of their status or how long they're perceived to stay in the country, they are offered a home and mandatory educational training under a devised system that would see the many young and adult uneducated and untrained new entrants, educated to a certain level and after which given period, they're equally trained on a profession of their choice. After a year to three years of such a deliberate planned effort to get them all committed into the system, by graduating from it would ensure those foreigners get sustained jobs and could establish their own businesses but would also understand the social nature of the societal structure and how to mesh with it.

This is particularly important amidst a wave of anti immigrant sentiments revving up around Europe such as in Sweden, where it's reported that suspected migrant gangs set alight over 100 cars in Gothenburg and other towns in the West Coast, in what Police say appeared to be coordinated attacks. A repeat of the 2013 arson attacks on cars and schools in Stockholm fueled by anger among second generation immigrants, at their perceived second-class status in that country. These immigrant foreigners and migrants are isolated in areas made exclusively for immigrants, and such areas termed 'a no-go zone' by far-right groups that keep emerging on regular basis, with one enemy in mind, "The foreign migrants and refugees." Sweden like other countries within the European Union have a huge migrant and refugees' population that remain idle. When would the government, employment agencies and business organizations recognize that keeping migrants on social welfare is not enough, and that more needs to be done to get everyone of this people economically integrated into the system. Educational literacy and employability skills in Swedish non-European immigrants would enable them to be able to contribute to the economy as it's difficult for non-citizens, not limited to Afghans and Somalians to find jobs in Sweden. This situation fuels idle minds and activities of criminal and drug gangs even terrorism, not only in Sweden but in Italy, Greece, Spain and Germany as well.

If the government of Germany, Sweden and others, recognize and appreciate the 'candle' in their insight, empathy and receptivity of this complex and responsible path they have taken due to their awareness of the plight of others as well as the beauty and strength rooted in the spirit of humanity and multiculturalism, and the follow-up active inclusion in the job market with analytical impact, I believe the nation's possibilities will be endless.

Moreover, many believe Germany isn't living to its full potentials as a powerful country. They could play an important role to lift Africa up or alongside China and could do it if they try harder. They could rain in investments backed up by an executive or legislative function to compel strong business organizations to invest in Africa and beyond to provide strong financial pillars and social responsibility that supports their sociopolitical stability and democracy. They could form or sponsor an advisory committee as delegation led by its head in the parliament to those countries to meet their heads of states to fashion out a way to improve the skills and employability ratio targeting the youths through training campaigns on various professions with the knowhow or intelligent support systems coming from Germany and their partners. Lastly, partnering with international finance organizations and African governments to liberalizing the act and framework to financial access including grants and loans to individuals in order to enable those already trained to build their platform on a nationwide deliberate, targeted and strategic approach meant to not just lift them out of poverty but to grow the bottom line of the country's economic index.

Not to mention, bring the media attention to the governments of the region to enhance a transparency to governance including the provision of health-care, social support services and fight against corruption. When it's all set and done, they could also claim all the glory based on the historical growth that might accrue from this holistic initiative.

Whatever it takes them to achieve that, they could ensure to the best of their ability, that it's done. In the end, the both parties will be happy for it because it will benefit everyone especially Europe who continue bickering, a situation that brings out the ugly head of the beast. But there are so many ways to tame that beast of racism, xenophobia, and bigotry and ensure it doesn't raise its ugly head ever again. Not in their streets, council meeting or the parliament, if they are strategic and long term in their approach to solve some of the basic economic and political problems facing Africa and Middle East including implementing ideas such as these.

If America is a land of immigrants, Germany itself can't escape that future. Ultimately, the future of Germany will be the immigrant future. Some Germans wouldn't like to entertain such an idea or reality, but it shouldn't be feared because it is a reality that would visit every nation on earth, it's a matter of time, unless of course humans live in outer space and not on earth. On earth, there are no borders and artificial borders can't stop a determined and miserable migrant to reaching and living in the country of his or her choice as he or she flees war, violence, persecution, and hunger. I have imagined it, may be, nature is restructuring the world to suit itself, the way nature has intended of it before humans started imposing their ignorant will on the earth. Barriers and fences are put to create artificial way of life and differences based on shape, color and race projecting laws and legislations that destroy the environment with selfish intentions and ambitions without long-term vision of its consequences. A situation that only benefit a few whiles the majority of others suffer. Who cares, if the guy in Somalia or Eritrea or even Syria dies of hunger, violence and explosion. We watch it on Television, and feel pity, at least for some.

For many others, the images which television have bombarded them with on daily basis, have managed to cause the opposite chain reaction draining out the love of humanity in people's hearts. So, what? Television is just what it is. Television, not a physical experience. A lot of people watch it like a movie and go home and sleep well. "Who does that?" When his neighbour is dying and screaming? At least what I learned in Germany is that the problem of your neighbour is also your problem. So, Germany of all, recognizes that fact as it sees a surge in migration from other European nationals into its country seeking for a good life, jobs and quality education for themselves and their families. "If that is not a position of privilege, tell me what it is?"

I often wonder about the forbearing and retrogressive phrase **"Illegal Migration"**. Why would anyone irrespective of their status and power use such an indulgent, doctrinal and intolerant phrase. The question is, is there any human that is illegal in a world where all humans are travelers? If politicians use that phrase I might easily overlook it on the grounds that these are hypocrites and self serving, egocentric dotards, preoccupied with their own interests and sucked up in their own little illusory fantasies as well as disregarding the reality of truth and International law. The question is, why would the organized objective Media or world press echo such unreceptive, stodgy and precocious prejudices coming from a place that is narrow minded, judgmental, intolerant neither considerate of others other than themselves when they recognized the sheer power their voice holds. The United States is in blatant breach of Article 31 of the Refugee Convention when it decides to impose penalties on asylum seekers for having illegally crossed its Southern border. The drafters of the Refugee and Asylum Law realized that no country including the United States gives refugee a visa to come make an asylum claim.

There's no other way to arrive other than illegally. There's no alternative for one in a hurry fleeing from war, persecution, extreme hunger, violence, organized crime and rape.

Media organizations and the free Press has an important role to play in all this. Addressing issues from the cause to where things presently stand while putting pressure on those governments and their global partners to act to proffer a permanent solution to challenges facing various nations around the globe. For example, the southwestern region of the Republic of Cameroon is burning. The French controlled government run by a dictatorial and despotic ruler who has been in power for over thirty-five years, has since the fall of the year 2017 been inhibiting and repressing the freedom of speech, expression and rights to protests by the indigenous English or Anglophone region of that country. Many are brutally tortured, restrained, severely beaten even as many others are killed by the military and houses of poor citizens of the southwest region burnt to ashes as tens of thousands flee into the South-South region of Nigeria to seek protection from cruel and draconian iron-fisted response from the oppressive military, political repression and death. All they seek is greater freedom to be represented in the national political governance and discourse of that country. Being under minded, they sought the right to self determination from the suppressive dominant and discriminative francophone who govern the country and plunged them to alienation and poverty. If they were given an equal hand to contribute to the development of the society, they may not have agitated for a separate state.

Of course, they took a cue from the Indigenous People of Biafra secessionist movement in Southeast Nigeria, their neighbours, which until it was blacklisted and crushed in 2017 by an arbitrary military offensive ordered by Mohammadu Buhari, the arrogant, tribalistic and democratic despot President of Nigeria, it stood for the same principles of freedom, justice and equality like their Cameroon counterparts. It intensified calls to breakaway from Nigeria a few months prior in 2017. The excluded fought back in a language of exclusion.

It could be recalled that the same long simmering tensions from the same marginalized ethnic group plunged Nigeria into one of the world's worst civil wars in recent memory between 1967-1970. A war that left over a million people dead of mostly the Igbo ethnic group. Parts of the unnerving and excruciating details were even captured in the Novel, titled; **"Half of a Yellow Sun"** by **Chimamanda Ngozi Adichie**

"Where is the Media exposure to all of this?" Where are all the big media stations to reporting the incessant torture and pain undergone by those poor people in Cameroon?" But the same media stations are quick to reiterate the positions of the western governments about how they feel about migrants coming to their nations or to report on how many desperate migrants and refugees are dying in the seas and risking their lives to go where they are not wanted. If they only try more, to covering the outrageous depraved violations and crimes against humanity going on there in their homeland, it could place the government in check and prevent further distressed situations urging refugee mass migrations of the agonizing people to places such as Europe where they are now largely not wanted.

America's populist Emperor Donald Trump could babble about deporting millions because of seeing their country in such a position of power, respected status and higher standard of living. A country that is blessed by God Himself like the handsome child among other not so cute brethren. While his crack down on immigrants may not seem to some as mass deportations but to many others especially those under the Axe, their relatives and friends, it feels so much like so. The administration attempts to cut down on legal immigration, return to the peak deportation levels or even surpass that of his predecessors, along with rhetoric and drive to act on them in recent months since taking office has sent the chills down the spine of many while loading fear into the immigrant population has made many to feel they could be rounded up, thereby making many to run to Canada before the Immigration and customs Enforcement could arrest them and ship them back to their homeland. The fear is based on the people who were already picked up and put into custody, those who were not previously targeted even under his predecessors.

Many who have called America home for decades are arrested and detained. By targeting legal migrants and refugees, America's Trump injects into the minds of some, the shuddering fear of themselves falling victims to the implacable misfortune of a cruel crackdown and arbitrary arrests in the hands of a legionary-ants ICE agents enabled by a toxic and inhumane ambience of a country ruled by an inexorable, unsympathetic and intolerant authoritarian wanna be Leader. A situation that is being viewed as mass deportation by the immigrant communities and the rest of the American citizens. Trump raves on all fronts to restrict migration or discourage further immigrants' entry into his country while projecting America First. In California, employers of labour who know the status of some of their workers as undocumented residents inform the Customs Enforcement agency (ICE) during court rulings or disputes over wages to enforce their oppressive mandate on undocumented employees under a climate poisoned with hate, discrimination and betrayal as well as maltreatment of foreign workers in America. In recent times, under an ever rising intolerant, bigoted and toxic atmosphere, the general question now asked in most rich societies relates to the status of a person such as: **"Where are you from?" "Are you illegal or undocumented?"** And not about the economic, mental state and social well-being of a person.

Recent published United States Immigration and Customs Enforcement (ICE) data shows that deportations of people arrested in the United States rose to 61,094 from January 20 to September 30th, 2017, compared to 44, 512 in the same period of 2016. According to the European Migration and Migrant Population Statistics, 2 Million non-EU citizens immigrated to the Eurozone in 2016. Foreign citizens made up 7.5 % of people living in the European Union Member States on 1st January 2017. European Member States granted citizenship to almost 1 Million persons in 2016. In 2016, there were 39,626 people who were removed from the United Kingdom or departed voluntarily after the initiation of removal. Nationals of India, Pakistan and Romania made up of 32 % of the 2016 deportations.

On the other hand, 37 % fewer non-EU citizens found to be illegally present in the European Union in 2017 compared with 2016. Almost 190,000 non-EU citizens were returned outside of the European Union in 2017, 17.4 % fewer than in 2016. Record number of non-EU citizens refused entry into the European Union in 2017 (440,000), the highest since 2009. In Germany, almost 22,200 people were deported to their home countries between January and November of 2017, according to the Federal Ministry of the Interior. In 2016, this figure was higher at a total of 25,400 people. Almost 30,000 refugees were said to have voluntarily left Germany in 2017 after many were rejected asylum.

In 2016 and 2017, from Afghanistan to Turkey, Ethiopia to Nigeria and the Balkan region, European Union were making struggling nations take back failed asylum seekers. These might just feel like numbers, but these were people who amid pain, frustration and grief were summoned, interrogated, cross-examined, on why they came, while being subjected to a state of uncertainty, fear, anxiety and mental torture until the day they were eventually sent out of the country. What a cruel modern world we live in?

The same migrant kid or young foreigner of today could aspire and excel in several areas of life by tomorrow such as sports, literature, commerce and even in the Technological and Innovation sector as seen in the life of Mark Zuckerberg, Founder of Facebook and Elon Musk, Founder of Tesla.

America and Germany with the position of privilege with blossoming economies such as that of Germany in 2016 and 2017 with so much surpluses, and loved by many for its model society including good road network, functional social structures, economic stability and beautifully diverse nation is that beautifully beloved and enviable progeny. How many have thought perhaps the immigrant wave of the past or recent migrants had something to do with it, perhaps zero or a few. According to official estimates, in 2016, Germany recorded the highest trade surplus in the world worth 310 billion dollars, making it the biggest capital exporter globally. In 2017, the country accounted for 28 percent of the Euro area economy, according to the International Monetary Fund. Many Germans want to believe Germany is successful because it works hard.

But an older friend of mine, well not really a friend. More like an acquaintance. He met me when I was writing my book in McDonald's restaurant and was interested in what I was doing. I said, I'm writing a book. "Really," he responded. In German or English, he asked. English, I answered. Where are you gonna sell the book?" He asked. "Online, in stores and everywhere where English is spoken including Germany. But it could also be translated into German, I hope it did. After all, the book is mostly about Germany", I replied him.

"Where do you come from?" You appear interesting, perhaps we could be friends, he asked. 'From Africa,' I replied. Nooo! Africa is big. What country? He asked again. Nigeria, I answered. They treat you guys bad and treat the middle Easterners better in this country. Not because they like them. It's just a matter of scale of preference. Bavarians are just bigots especially the politicians. They don't like any other people but themselves. They think they're better of than other parts of their country. They play divisive politics" he added. I like Africans, my wife is African, from Namibia, he said to me. What are you writing about, he asked. "A literature about the nature of the current migration, its causes, European Union's role in addressing those global issues, America and the future of the world, from a careful study of the present times, its *handwriting* on the *wall* and interpreting them in a way that would be understood as history and current affairs wrapped up around experiences and testimonies from about fifty people interviewed," I expounded my ideas. "Do you know Germans think, they are the drivers of their economy?" They must be deluded to think that. Without migrants and the immigrant population in Germany from the start, this country is nothing. I say it all the time to everyone I meet, he responded to me with sincerity of heart.

"Tell me about Nigeria, please," he asked. Nigeria is a multi lingual, multiethnic and multicultural country. I'd always thought the biblical *"Tower of Babel"* fell in that country especially in the Southern part bordering Southwest Cameroon where the 'Bantu' civilization originated and expanded from. There's a popular song lyric in Nigeria that says, *"every kilometer is another language."* The country is diverse. For clarity, the "Bantu" civilization is not only recognized in known history to have conquered the entire sub-Saharan continent, and building some of the greatest ancient structures, of which ruins are standing up to this day, such as the great West African Monoliths and the Great Zimbabwean lost civilization but recent research and findings placed this old tribe as more than just largely Hunter gatherers, as they might have been the settlers and founders of the Egyptian civilization including the Sumerian, Babylonian, Assyrian and the Hittites. Their earliest migration patterns may have played a role in their level of societal structure, enlightenment and development through the Southern Sahara starting about 4,500-3,000 B.C. From the language patterns, to the needle stone carved and the triple concentric artistically designed Monoliths to their prophetic worship of the Sun and Storm deity called 'BA,' which reflects similar features found throughout the Middle East such as BA'AL, or BEL. Wilhelm Bleek's coinage of the term BANTU in 1857 was inspired by the prefix 'Ba', after observing the dominant verbal use of the Ba, throughout the cultures of Africa.

The prefix O'BO, O'BU, M'BA, A'BE, O'BA, A'BA representing BA'AL or BEL which signifies Lord applied to various gods in the Mesopotamian religion of Akkad, Assyrian and Ba'bylonian. In Greek, it's Belus. Linguistically, BEL is an easy Semitic form cognate with Northwest Semitic BA'AL with the same meaning. The God BEL was the chief God of Palmyra in pre-hellinistic times, worshipped alongside Aglibol or A-Ibol. A'Ibol is a similar name used for the Ibo tribe, a Bantoid language family from this area, who were taught to have re-migrated back from the Middle East after the fall of the first and second Jewish temple. The Jews or ancient Hebrew Israelites themselves were said to have emerged from the Canaanites, of which their God was BA'AL. Canaan himself was a descendant of Ham. The Ham descendants and civilization have found its ruins among the ancient 'Nok culture' that is said to have begun about 1500 B.C., in the area now known as Nigeria. The Bantu names like Yak' ubu or A-Ba'ssey in Niger-Delta, O'bama in Swahili and Ba'ndile in Kwazulu are still used all over sub-Saharan Africa. Earlier I mentioned "Babel," now I think there's a connection.

The "Nsibidi" hieroglyphs of the Bantoid family, as a system of symbols indigenous to what is now Southeastern Nigeria and Southwest Cameroon, maybe a key or missing link to connect that ancient civilization, and that of the Ba'bylonian cuneiform and ancient Egyptian hieroglyphic writing. The Nsibidi hieroglyphics of the Leopard society of West Africa connected to Osiris, the God founder of the Egyptian civilization, with similar patterns as those in Egyptian temples, are said to have appeared on excavated pottery and in ceramic stools and headrests from Calabar region with a range of dates from 400 to 1400 C.E. There are thousands of Nsibidi symbols, of which over 500 are recorded. Even, the name of the country Haiti or Haitian given to it by the European slave traders founded with slaves emanating from this region may be an actual name suggesting that the ancient Hittites or Haittic were of the same earlier origin, who at the twilight of their civilization re-migrated back across the Sahara to settle in West Africa. Clearly, the Bantu tribes may have been preceded by an older A'BA civilization that thrived South of the Atlantic Ocean coast, in what is today known as the equatorial warm temperate rainforest region of Central West Africa. Consequently, further archeological evidence targeting that region would be able to establish that fact.

So, you're saying, "what we know of the world's oldest civilizations including the Egyptian civilization was an offshoot of the Bantu family tribe earlier nestled around the Nigeria region?" he inquired further. Precisely, that's what I'm saying. My research analysis points to that fact.

Coming back to your question of modern Nigeria. One would say, they're all black and the same. But that's not the true picture. The only language that brings the country together is English and Pidgin English language. When I looked online, I realized that Nigeria came in third, on the list of countries with the most spoken indigenous languages behind Papua New Guinea and Indonesia. But I could've sworn it holds the world's largest ethnic groups occupying a small space especially in the Southern region. It's supposed to be the source of our strength, but no, it's not. In Nigeria, that's the major source of our division. The country is rich in human and natural resources including tin, copper, iron ore, gold, crude oil, cocoa, cotton, cassava, oil palm and coffee, but that is another part of the curse. As the discovery of crude oil and its exploration brought hope to many Nigerians and West Africans. But years into it, Nigeria abandoned agricultural production and its investments and focused on only crude oil. The cheap money corrupted those in power as autocratic leaders looted the Nation's treasury even as social infrastructures degenerated and more people became poorer with crippling sanctions that grinded the country to a halt. It was not until the year 1999, that democracy was instituted into the country and people hoped life in the country will change for the better.

True, while the country has changed in some ways since then with thriving financial institutions, Film, Music and Fashion industries, more of the country remains unchanged and poor. In 2018, it was named the country with the poorest people on Earth. That couldn't be truer, seeing the number of young people migrating out of the country in search for a better life. That's a brief history of my country, Nigeria. Hmmm! Holistic, interesting, he replied. I predict your book will be a bestseller, as he smiled. It was nice meeting you. He dropped off his card with me saying call me if you can and moved to board his flight almost immediately. After he left, I thought to myself that was a man who speaks the truth. Many Germans are like that because they have seen the shady and gray side often in its own people and could care less speaking the truth in not just issues that are personal to them but the generality of others including foreigners that are often despised, scorned or discriminated against, in a climate of anti immigrant sentiments that started long before 2015, but effectively from that year when they was the wave of mass migration of Syrians and others into Germany.

What would German people have thought will be the reaction of their Chancellor? Perhaps, they would have wanted her to say, "Send them back, we don't want them." Maybe, but Angela Merkel was different because she recognized the position she occupies and don't want history to judge her wrong or treat her legacy with disrepute. Just like many people say one thing in the public and another thing behind the walls like flatulent, stage-managing and double-faced cowards. But I thought she was unfeigned in her firm expression when she said those historically defining words, 'Wir Schaffen Es', meaning "We can do it." Germany is strong, we can pull it off. She was speaking about Germany, its muscle to shoulder the burden and its prosperous future with all its surpluses which entered a new next level in that year and after the 2015 migrants wave but to be honest, she didn't go to Syria to tell Syrians, "I urge you to come to Germany, it is good over here." No, she did what any mother and leader in her position would do in accordance with International law and in contrast to the history her country and Europe witnessed in the 1930s and 1940s during the second world war.

I believe she was honest, but that honesty would cost her, her party's dominant position as the far-right party captivated the fearful on the back of bigotry, capitalizing in their sentiments against her policies to rise to power. I mean, 'Alternative for Germany,' (AfD), they call it. And recently the Bavarian Party Christian Social Union, the so-called conservative CDU sister party who were fighting her and her migrant's policy from the inside threatening to close the Southern border to migrants if she doesn't comply with their demands to send migrants back especially those already processed in their first point of entry into Europe. As well as urging a quick legislation of policies to expedite the deportations of migrants and refugees denied stay in their state and country. The question is, is she the only sane political animal in that country and in a cranky Europe that have since 2015 saw a rise in populist party movements and peevish leaders rise to power from Austria, Poland to recently Italy. As a foreigner myself, I'm waiting to see, perhaps the very day she's out of office, the humane heart and well grounded sensible head alongside her counterpart, the French President, her seat might be taken by a far-right or right-wing populist politician who may have indulged and indoctrinated the country's like minded populace in down low rhetoric to see their own side of the story of how foreigners or illegal migrants, as they call them, come to fester and spoil their cherished culture or valued way of life.

It's hard to know if she regretted her stance and actions later for the toll and not so good an impact her open-door policy had on her image and her liberal conservative party, the Christian Democrats (CDU). But at least she did the right thing. She got her reward while in office during her third term in office as she was deemed the most powerful woman in a row and the in defacto leader of the free world, in the absence of the real leadership from America, and her leader Donald Trump who came to power by selling bigotry, narcissism, racism and xenophobia in his country. I'd always thought America don't belong to those ignorant people who don't truly know its history or knew but would rather prefer to ignore it. *If they are true owners of the country called the 'United States of America,' it should be the 'African Americans' because they toiled with their sweat and blood to establish it, while the other true owners of the land are the Native Americans because they are the earlier settled occupants of the land long before the Europeans discovered it.* Perhaps, if it was possible to deport those two groups of minorities in his country out elsewhere because of how they look or his perception of them, he could have done so from day one. The typical expression of white power and their claim of superiority in everything in that country.

This exact situation happened in Australia as the European Australians believed that their civilization was superior to that of the indigenous Australians, based on their color and comparative technological advancement. The minority communities were marginalized, their voices silenced, rights restricted while their lands were taken away from them. The physical disadvantages they suffered remain unchanged. Life expectancy is for indigenous Australians ten years less than the white population. The unemployment rate is four times higher. The child mortality rate is twice as much. Moreover, the aboriginal Australians are incarcerated at a higher rate than any other suppressed group on earth. Twenty-seven percent of the adult prisoners are aborigines while making up just three percent of the population. Many arguing throughout the twentieth century that everything must be done to convert the stolen generation of the mixed descent children into white citizens. The adherents of these beliefs considered any proliferation of mixed descent children to be a threat to the nature and stability of the prevailing civilization or racial evolving heritage.

In 2013, then Prime Minister Kevin Rudd, declared no man, no woman, or child who sought asylum in Australia by boat would ever be allowed to settle in the country, regardless of whether they had family there. Until its closure in late 2017, detention centres for refugees and asylum seekers were set up in Manus Island where over a thousand people were held as the sea waters were patrolled and trolled by the Australian navy who tracks boats of refugees coming from Southeast Asia, captures and sends back fleeing migrants right back to their home countries. The controversial and much criticized immigration policy of Australia ignored reports of the poor state of its basic infrastructure to allegations of torture and mismanagement with astonishing rates of traumas, mental illnesses and up to six deaths until Papua New Guinea ultimately ruled its existence illegal in the fall of 2017. In 2015, more than 500 men began a two-week hunger strike in protest against the prolonged detention and conditions on the Island. This in addition to the 2015 reports revealing widespread healthcare failings provided in the detention centres. At the heart of the policy is a single goal meant to stop asylum seekers from traveling to Australia by Boats.

I'd like to believe in the wisdom of the folklore, common ideology or African myth that says the time of the rise of Africa effectively started in 1914 and probably by the end of the 21st century (2100) and beyond, Africa would rise and be leading the world as not just as a united economic power bloc but would become the *'Only Super Power Region On Earth or Wakanda forever...'* If you may. A position enjoyed by the United States of America for almost two centuries. Upon this great future, it would project true, unrivaled and uncompetitive strength grounded in oneness without regard to culture, language, traditional values, race, creed, color of skin, stereotypes, class, language, ethnicity and religion, as religion will be the last doctrinal human moral controlling power to dissolve into the character of the prevailing new paradigm and elevated consciousness within the conscious awareness of a communal universal Brotherhood, and so is the concept of the 'State,' with its land, boundary, territory, sovereignty, its body of rules and laws.. This unified future world system of governance established under a new powerful, broader and respected United Nations Organization World governing body or 'World Federation' will insure economic growth, peace and security to all nations and people, different from what the world knows now. They will exist and operate using the principles of a redefined universal laws of life, love, experience, knowledge, service, expansion, time and space leading to a broader and more profound social, mind, ethical and behavioral changes and consequences while melting polarity in a new balance to create a new peaceful society in all places of the **One True Future Earth**.

Whether it's an unrealistic myth or fairy tale, who cares? The world agrees 'Africa is the future' with a collective rebirth or major awakening of the world's future model as hoped by many thinkers to begin essentially from the year 2030 to 2065. As long as that future could bring hope to the ordinary African who'll think it's not worth it taking a dangerous journey across the Sahara to a place or region other than their country or continent, hoping to secure a future that isn't guaranteed, then it's a good thing. That year 1914 in particular was of importance as it marked the beginning of a new rebirth in human thinking not just for Africa but the world, as the world experienced great positive benefits accrued in areas such as technology, boost in science and new medical discoveries after the first world war. The League of Nations was formed to prevent wars where conflicts will be settled through diplomacy and an international organization devoted to peace.

More over, there was a greater acceptance of women after the 1914 war, as before that time the suffragette movement was stagnated as the war gave an opportunity for women to take on roles or jobs previously done by men only. That year proved a significant factor in giving women the vote in 1919 and helped changed social attitudes towards women forever. In this context, it's seen as a war for freedom of global consequence and enlightenment. Between the 1860s and early 1900s after the era of the transatlantic slavery, Africa faced imperialist aggression, diplomatic pressures, military invasions, eventual conquests and colonization. After the 1914 first world war, humanitarian ideas were common. Humanitarianism came not only from the antislavery movement and a general idea of fairer treatment for the African natives, but colonial powers also realized that by taking care of the welfare of the inhabitants of Africa, it would lead to greater productivity.

Therefore, moral principles came to a head as new ideas and practices evolved. Doors were opened for a mandate system of self rule among African natives to be promoted and consequently implemented leading to independence of African nations after the second world war, which strengthened the ideals for freedom and development started few decades earlier. It was not necessary for the wars to occur but by occurring because of the European empires quest for power, it led to a broader sense of justice, unity and freedom for all.

To further elucidate on this fact, according to the '**science of the lost cycle of time,**' the ancient cultures around the world spoke of a vast cycle of time with alternating dark and enlightenment ages. Plato called it the Great year. Many old cultures believed consciousness and history are not linear but cyclical, the rising and falling of things over long periods of time. The folklore of over thirty ancient cultures, which the African Bantu tribes including Yoruba Culture in West Africa as one of them, speak of a cycle of time with long periods of enlightenment broken by dark ages of ignorance, indirectly influenced by a known astronomical phenomenon; "The Procession of the Equinox." There are two celestial motions: 'Diurnal Motion' and 'Earth's rotation of its axis,' that have profound effect on life and consciousness, causing humans to move from a waking state to a sleep state, and back again every twenty-four hours.

Our bodies have adapted to this rotation, so well that it produces these regular changes in consciousness without our thinking the process as remarkable. The earth's revolution around the sun which Copernicus identified, has a significant effect on life, prompting trillions of life forms to spring out of the ground, to bloom, fruit and then decay. Our visible world springs to life, changes its color and stride, then reverses with every waxing and waning of the second celestial motion. The third celestial motion called the "Procession of the Equinox," is less understood, but according to ancient cultures it's equally trans formative. What disguises the impact of this motion is its Timescale. The humans have an average life span that comprises of one-360th of the roughly twenty-six-thousand-year processional cycle. The idea of the great cycle linked to the slow procession of the equinox was common to the numerous ancient cultures leading to the great era of Christianity, the place where it started from and the empire that anchored it. This time line has guided the rise and fall of many other known civilizations of the past starting from the Sumerian, Egyptian, Babylonian, Persian, Greece to the Roman empire civilization even to the rise of the New world of America. This time period, no matter how long or short is usually marked by a larger than life figure like a Messiah who fights, frees and leads the people to a new golden era. For example, for the Egyptian civilization, the New

Kingdom of Giza was founded and fathered by "Osiris," the God of the Orion sky and the underworld as their Teacher. In Greek civilization, it was the God of Thunder, "Zeus," the Highest. His children founded the Grecian city states including Athens while Alexander, The Great, the human Son of Zeus united and led it to global power and prominence. The Roman Empire had Julius Caesar who was elevated to the place of a God, as the human representative for Jupiter after his death. Christianity had "Jesus Christ" as its forebear, while, for the American continent, it was "Columbus," as its Pathfinder. The United States Masons particularly exalted "George Washington" to the level of a God representing Osiris and his Orion belt symbol of the three sun stars appearing in Washington D.C. flag, as the one who led the fight to give that country its independent nationhood opening up the path for a free, fair and democratic state marked by a brilliant destiny that is engineered by the future of technology and creativity rendering unbelievable prosperity. The question is, "who will be the *Hero of the coming African golden age?*" My Best guess will probably point to the Black Panther (The return of the Leopard God Osiris) or Superman (Sun-God Horus/The Christ), or both. We'll see!

This is where it gets interesting. According to astronomical and archaeological evidence, the understanding of its ebbs, flows, and character of each epoch provides insight into the direction of where the new civilization will emerge from, being a renaissance or rise of a new wave of consciousness sparking enlightenment and of course the place, country or continent that will berth this shining light. The same vision of destiny and empirical evidence over a period spanning several centuries show that the next big long-term civilization shift or ray of enlightenment and hope will undoubtedly emanate from the " HEART OF AFRICA", back to the Eden, if you may call it so; to where it all started, in the first place after about 6,000 years of being at the center of the world. It's a shame we are not taught all these, in the secondary school. What's more, when the new renaissance finally awakes in the cradle as 'Africa,' it may remain there for a long time beyond a 500- or 1000-years era. A time period that would enable it to come to full perfection. This might trigger a major shift in consciousness, body of knowledge, cooler and shape of not just the earth, its life forms or universe itself but physiological, biological and mental changes seen and felt in the material bodies, molecular DNA and behavioral characteristics of humans throughout the earth plane. It's estimated that by the year 3,000 AD, the entire humans in all regions of the earth will go completely "BLACK", having one language. The Igbo cultural folktale predicted that the "waters" that took the transatlantic slaves will bring them back when all things are fulfilled, and the time of Africa arrives. But added that they'll not come back alone.

Imagine, a white nationalist belonging to Neo Nazi sleeping and waking up at that time, a thousand years from now, looking at his skin, he will definitely cry. These illuminations of the Procession of the Equinox predicted the rise of China and other Eastern powers as a rival to the United States to strike an equilibrium while taking the world to the pedestal of a predetermined outcome but noted explicitly, 'IT' will not replace 'IT.'

I am a Libra, and according to the providence of justice and equilibrium prevalent in our sign, we believe in fairness and the equality of persons with the belief we all are equal as created by God Almighty. We are all one. I believe they should be no artificial borders, no discrimination, xenophobia, racism, sexism or bigotry because the world is beautiful this way. It is without artificial imprints or super imposition over the laws of nature. Regardless of the times, past or present, the end is not always good looking for anyone group or race held higher or powerful over others. That brutal mind set, its principles and the strong reaction to it has torn our world apart over the years and centuries past, and that foolishness should end now. It is not human neither is it in our nature to be discriminative. Firstly, we are one. People often misconstrue its meaning. In that phrase, I think it means, you are me and I am you. In a man, there's a woman and inside a woman exist a man. Equally, inside a white person is a black being, and inside a black person exists a white person. There's no difference between us. That's how I interpret it to mean. Unless of course, there are other interpretations to it or how every school of thought interpret it to mean. The truth is, we are more alike than we know and together we are stronger. Unity in diversity.

Everyone needs his or her space at one time or another. It is easy to feel overwhelmed like people saying; *"Oh there are just too many of them coming to our city and country. That happens in up to 90 percent of the population, but research has also shown that the same amount of people or even more are against any attempt aimed at attacking, insinuating, disparaging, labeling, stereotyping and discriminating even deporting those migrants and asylum seekers back to their home land."* Because they themselves know, that no man is an island. One day, they might find themselves in another country which is all so developed and would want to seek refuge or permanent residence, and they would want the people in that future different country to be nice to them, receptive and not reject them. It's the law of nature to do unto others the way thou desire to be done to thee. It's called, put your self in my shoe. "Whoever knew China or Dubai would rise they way it did and in such a fast pace at the shortest possible time? What then stops one from believing that in the future perhaps from the 2030s and beyond, African nations will once again emerge as the fastest growing economies on earth and that might continue until Africa reaches a point of sustainable development?" An economically viable and unified block without artificial barriers for Asia, Europe and America to trade with, with profitable returns! "Or, don't you think it's possible?" The world goes around, and no position of power is permanent. It's either you leave or die in that position or the power will fleece from your grabs. It's one or the other or none. Either way, nothing is permanent in this temporal journey of life where a young man or woman in a few years becomes wrinkled. The next time you see the same person might be in his or her grave. In a broader perspective, say the space or universe, this concept is called "Arrow of Time" and "Entropy." The moment of big bang or beginning to the point where all things wanes and eventually collapses. These changes occur from the atoms in the quantum level to the stars and black holes in the macro universe. You're a fool to think otherwise. If it's impossible to elongate one's life with the mystery of eternal life because it eludes one, how do one then think one could control time and the changes it brings not just to him or her as a person and the evolution of consciousness, but to organizational entities, cities and destiny of nations and the world at large.

Sometimes nature bruises your ego and it doesn't care. When the time comes anything, and everything happens sometimes without a warning defying plan and strategy. And that is the scariest part. There are no Hollywood happy endings. No, nothing of such in real life because we deal with the reality of nature itself which can be kind or harsh. Those double realities constitute the future of everyman. We all are used to it as it governs our every aspects of life from our personal life to the professional life up even to the weather patterns and the seasons. Nothing stays the same.

It's a matter of time, all things change or reverses it course. It's natural and always the position of time and privilege of everything that exist under the sun to experience change for better or worst whether we like it or not. That feeling gives hope to the suffering people that one day things would improve and his or her pain and anguish would finally have an end. Once again looking back at my journey and the journey of many other immigrants, suffering migrants, refugees and asylum seekers seeking a peaceful and better life over the years to countries such as this one, "Germany", there's one thing all have in common including the host country and that is our common humanity and our ability to rise above our limitations, failures, trials, biases and differences to forge a common destiny that benefits all of us in spite of where we come from or cultural orientation. Whether good policies have helped to secure such a future for all especially in Germany, posterity shall tell! As history shows integration helps not the foreigner but the host nation. Yet integration is the least of the worries and effort in the enacting of policies and promoting a lifestyle among citizens that would aid everyone to get to that level of thinking where we don't have to tolerate others because they're different be it their color, language or culture but to actually see everyone equally the same and one as us.

I read an article in *'The Telegraph,'* **"How Germans have fallen back in love with Hitler."** It has to do with a Novel published in 2011, titled; "Er ist wieder da" meaning "Look Who's Back" by Timur Vermes, where a dead Adolph Hitler resurrected in 2011 Berlin and proceeds to rise to prominence. The book became a bestseller in 2012. In the opening pages Hitler is surprised to see the city still standing. During his last days in the bunker, he gave instructions for everything to be destroyed. Not just houses but doors too. Also, door's handles. The screws, not only the long ones. The screws must be unscrewed and ruthlessly bent out of shape. The doors must be ground to sawdust, and then burnt to cinders." It's praised by its fans to be hilarious and funny. A German best seller sold 1.3 million copies beating Dan Brown's Novel on the German bestseller lists. The book's success is the more surprising given it was written in the same style as "Mein Kampf", the real Hitler autobiographical manifesto, which was itself effectively banned in Germany, along with Nazi symbols such as the Swastika. The story serves up the punchlines; what irritates me most about these morning people is their horribly good temper, as if they have been up for three hours, and already conquered France," Hitler grumbles at one point.

In another passage he compares a man operating a leaf blowing machine to SS men obeying their orders: "Even though they could have easily complained, what are we to do with all these Jews?'

It makes no sense anymore; They are being delivered faster than we can load them into gas chambers." Most Germans initially ignored the Book as reviews were mixed. Even the left-wing Tageszeitung slammed it as being dead boring." Other critics took issue with Hitler's fictional endearing qualities. Too often, the author depicts Hitler as a funny chap, and that ultimately has the effect of making things seem more harmless than they were, wrote the Sud-deutsche Zeitung. Vermes himself said in refusing to portray Hitler as a monster explains why so many Germans helped him, and whether they now might have done the same. You are thrown off course a bit because you think it's possible for someone like Hitler to be attractive. There are instances where you'd say, he's kind of right.

This gobbling ecstasy manifesting itself in fiction or reality does of course not end with book lovers, and their imagination to chose to love Hitler or resurrect his memories in a fantasy appealing way, the way they do now laughing at all the atrocities he committed, which many in Germany at the time helped and supported. In the social circles and among social groups not just the neo-Nazis who fly their flags on the streets of East Germany protesting the policies of the current administration and how soft Germany has become and are trying so hard to bring back the old days. But alongside, are other groups like the "Alternative for Germany" in suits inside the nation's parliament, alongside liberals making laws that targets these foreigners, whom they so much dislike. Though, they may consider themselves fighting for the rights of the ordinary German with hardline nationalistic view point and service to the citizen over the migrants and refugees, but they find that their actions are directly or indirectly fueling another dimension of a poisoned and alienated radical groups who are tired with their lives and are looking for those foreigners to vent their anger upon. *Some moderate Germans still maintain that racism is gravely buried in the fabric of the society. It's a time bomb waiting for the right time to express itself in a not so pretty way.*

This informs the reason why Asylum centres or refugee hostels were set on fire by racially-motivated hating arsonists while grenades were thrown at refugees and asylum seekers hostel in Villingen-Schwenningen, a repeat of the 1992 refugees hostel fire bomb attack in Karlsruhe by Neo-Nazi. In October 2015, after the event of the mass migration into Germany upsetting the right-wing groups, there were 576 offenses targeting refugees' hostels and individuals in Germany as reported by the Police. Many refugees were attacked whether in the public or at nights with violence meted against them including funny name calling in public places or in social gatherings.

In situations, where these have happened, all some local authorities could say was to blame refugees and asylum seekers for being what they are. Also, blaming the recent administration's policy of allowing migrants and refugees into their land for causing a rise in these hardline movements as well as a stir in the childish or hateful mindset of the radicals spurring deviants such as these, to malicious attacks against those they suspect to be migrants, refugees or foreigners as a whole who don't look like them. *"Of all those number of cruel racists arsonists in 2015 and 2016 possibly deciphered by the Police, how many of them were punished for such a serious crime?" Or, are we living in a new communist East Germany reality all over again, when foreigners especially those with dark skinned were lynched or killed without repercussion to them or justice to those harmed while evidences were covered up by the Police under an atmosphere poisoned by the politics of hate?*

Perhaps that's the scenario the current Chancellor Angela Merkel is trying so hard to avoid, a repeat of the mistakes of the past, because by tolerating a nascent hardline ideology of nationalism or bigotry, it could in the end accumulate and mutate into something else that can't be tamed or controlled. That's why she continues to be a humanist by trying to make her people, her fellow politicians and European leaders realize the ordeals, pain and suffering undergone by these migrants, who are first of all, people, who came in from war zones such as Syria or those who journeyed through the Sahara desert and faced all kinds of unimaginable things, many of whom lost their lives over the Mediterranean sea, over thirty thousand people approximately since the last seventeen years, and then reaching the European shores, a place they hope to find peace, love and a better life, only to be hated, asked to go back or not welcomed in Europe. She realized that by echoing the voices of the many or few who attack or detest refugees and asylum seekers like a plague or unwanted strain doesn't make her better than them, and this had led her severally to often stand alone in calling for the rest of Europe to tolerate, accept and share the burden equally of resettling the migrants and refugees once they're in Europe. Remember a migrant or refugee coming to Europe after such ordeals doesn't make everything fine or their problems suddenly go away as some suffer from a degenerative permanent brain disorder or psychological injury and mental illness that often go without a cure.

More than that, these migrants and asylum seekers have to deal with excruciating bureaucratic bottlenecks with jagged heart stinging letters or correspondence from the migration and refugees department that control them like puppets, some for the rest of their stay in Europe. A situation where they are dragged from one migration office to another for asylum case assessment or review or the other. All culminating in incessant needless, judiciary court reviews and often failures based not on critical examination of evidence but old cultural prejudices. They often complain of the psychological stress and mental degradation; this needless process puts them through. Of course, under today's heated arguments of migration, where everyone is being watched and careful in their approach towards the refugees and migrant issue, expect that they'll be rejected no matter how convincing their testimony or evidence is presented. Then, there's the aspect of these people beginning a new life in Europe as they have to learn to adapt to a strange culture and tradition, that is unlike what they have experienced or known back at home. They have to learn the language. Of course, not everyone is talented to learn another language fast, as some spend the rest of their stay learning to speak German even as they are rejected in social organizations and denied jobs or employment just because their Deutsch is not good enough. And the aspect of mingling in social circles or learning to know their neighbours or entering into relationships, or when employed in the labour sector, would remind or teach them a whole new lesson that they are completely existing on an entirely new template and separate bubble or are different from their German counterparts either at work or in close relationships, and must begin life as "Born Again."

Many of the anti-immigrant sentiments are based on the fact that not just Germany or ignorant parts of it, but Austrians, English, polish, Italians, Hungarians wants to keep, their white societies white while demoting the concept of multi-nationalism and equality to that of a special status of consideration. Just like the State of Israel recently did, as the Knesset passed a new law that elevates Israel as an exclusive nation of the Jews, Jerusalem as its Capital and Hebrew as their official language while Arabic is demoted to a special status. No mention of equality, minority rights and Democracy.

Just as well, Europeans are increasingly following the way of America's Trump. They don't favour or curry multiculturalism as they say, that concept doesn't work for all nations. That notion is of course tricky and deceptive in a multi party Union Bloc like the European Union. For the very fact that a nation in Europe agrees to be part of the European Union 28-member bloc means that country has resigned itself or fate to the rules governing the Union which are by the way freedom of movement of goods and people among the nations within this union. But also, the freedom for anyone to choose to live wherever he or she wants to live in. As well known every country within this Union is different having unique cultural differences that are sometimes quite remarkable as apart from the fact that they are mostly white nations, these cultural major differences, would qualify for multiculturalism. Just like a Polish man would wish to live in the United Kingdom even though that country is made up of people from various nations, continents, cultures and backgrounds that don't correlate but the land itself is a melting pot of cultures for all. People can practice their religions and beliefs as long as it doesn't infringe on other people's rights or cause dissent.

Outside the perimeter of the European Union such as in the United States, people can be black or Asian and live side by side in Los Angeles or in New York as a place to raise a family, for studies or for work, and they agree because the country they find themselves in, promotes tolerance and unity in diversity at least in the last century or mostly before Trump came in. The same can be said about the European Union as not only Europeans live in the Union as even the history of Europe show that Arabs and Africans have been living there for centuries. In recent twentieth century migrations, countries such as the United Kingdom has seen a rise in the number of Caribbean and Africans such as Trinidad and Tobago, Jamaica, Nigeria, Ghana, Kenyans and Zimbabwe, as well as Indians, Pakistanis, Australians and South East Asians living side by side with the traditional whites in that country.

The interesting part is that these nations immigrants live in the United Kingdom peacefully as long as their religion or ethnicity don't infringe on the rights and values of their host nation, or the British citizens themselves not resenting the very sight of those blacks or Indians they see on their streets. "Once again, if there's a history of other cultures in Europe spanning generations, living side by side with fellow Europeans for a long time, how come now all of a sudden, due to the rise in migration in recent years of people fleeing wars, persecution and violence, there'll be a problem, or make the Europeans in countries like Poland or Hungry or Czech republic not to feel like Europeans anymore?" Western Europe has always been a multiculturalist society, and it was those values that enabled the creation of the Union with the basic human values saddled with the rights to freedom and liberty of all, to live together and see themselves as one, as well as visitors or tourists having the pleasure and privilege to see everything and enjoy their stay within a United Europe that welcomes and accepts them.

Like one politician puts it, Europe is playing a card of populism in order to appeal to their constituencies, so that their voters don't go and vote for other parties in next elections. Apart from Germany and the western European nations, unemployment is on the rise in some Southern and Eastern European nations like Hungary, Greece, Poland and the Balkan states even Italy. Foreigners and migrants become scapegoats when jobs are scarce. In addition to the already depressing political environment, Europe has about twenty million Muslims, some of whom are feared under the present climate. But to be sure, they are indigenous Turks in Germany, many of whom have contributed in the rebuilding of the country after the second world war.

Pakistanis in the United Kingdom and Arabs of mostly African descent in France. But they share one common denominator: They are all marginalized. They are sometimes targeted as potential Islamic terrorists. Some argue that the challenge is Integration. But is integration possible without Multiculturalism? But in Multiculturalism based on Integration, one has to give some and take some. Most western societies want that foreigners should give up everything in-order to integrate while assimilating their new culture. If that happens, then it's not multiculturalism, as that concept allows for all foreigners in Europe to still practice their religions and cultures side by side with the host nation citizens, as long as their activities are not a malaise to their host nations. Unfortunately, this stance is reinforced by the recent migration under a political climate that look as if they are pushed to the wall and are fighting back from the brink. Politicians spew poison by reinforcing political hostility towards the new migrants and asylum seekers with doctrinal arguments rooted in old prejudices.

Immigration and mass movements are on the rise both within and from outside the European Union. Migrants actively contribute to the economic, social and cultural development of the European Union and its diverse societies. The key to ensuring the best possible outcomes for both the migrant and the European Union is for true integration and inculcating the principles of multiculturalism into host countries as a guiding principle to constituting and re-branding itself as the New Europe, a future they can't deny or escape from. Member states must develop and strengthen their integration policies with room for the immigrant, migrants and refugees to breathe, even as they build the pillars of a new spirit of oneness to support education, employment, access to social services and active participation in the host societies. Whether it's economic, cultural or humanity, the new framework has the capacity to transform the void created by the lack of trust while ushering in benefits that promote a powerful diverse continent with other enrichments that have for too long remain undervalued.

Once again, the European Union must see a way of protecting foreigners, refugees and migrants, not only those within or those born into it and are facing discrimination, racial bias or hate but those who on daily basis strive to reach its frontiers from all fronts especially through the sea. Statistics from the International Organization for Migration show that more than 4,000 boat migrants died in the year 2012 and 2013. In 2014, 3,270 migrants perished in the sea and more than 3,770 died in 2015. This reveals that migration routes through the Mediterranean have become the most dangerous in the world. Such dreadful figures under stark reality of anguish faced by desperate refugees and migrants are not just data but deal with real people. The data also show the reality of suffering, desperate risky journey and the failure of policy by the European Union and the International community to protect poor people who flee persecution, crisis, violence and poverty to make a new life in their region. They were shipwrecks almost regularly occurring in the sea as a consequence of the failure of the European Union and its member states as well as their policies to protect refugees.

But as they were constantly presented with these challenges, they merged immigration and asylum, with the aim of controlling irregular flow of migrants in their border. By so doing they were not doing their duty of protection of the sea but rather with a new goal of border management and migration control. Instead of preventing deaths in the sea, they were geared at preventing migrant crossing to their borders. Frontex was formed on this regard, the European agency for migration management and operational cooperation at the external borders of the member states. Their activities increased after 2015. The commission supported plans in the European agenda on migration and the European Union action plan against migrant smuggling (2015-2020). It was learned that the council launched a military operation that aims to disrupt the business model of human smuggling and trafficking networks in the Southern Central Mediterranean. However, what all these measures have brought was the detaining of refugees in holding cells in Libya, brutal slave like treatment meted on the innocent migrants, insufficient support to the Libyan coast guards that do little to arrests smugglers and protect the fleeing migrants and the ineffectiveness or failure of Frontex to patrol the sea to the southern front close to Libya, leading to the deaths of migrants unabated in the sea. In the era of the rising of populist governments in the European Union and their agitation fueled by party politics to restrict or end migration of people coming into their countries' borders, the aid agencies that have been helping to do the work that could have been done by Frontex, are disparaged, and their work of saving lives is reduced to subversive detraction of their policies of limiting migration flows.

And although, thousands of people were in the fall of 2017 and early 2018, collected from this holding cells and flown back to their individual countries including Nigeria, Niger, Cameroon, Ghana, Senegal and north Africa, etc., after a CNN documentary exposed the horrors of migrant auction and forced labour, triggering an outcry all over the world, migration across the Sahara to Libya has not stopped even as the business of trafficking continues to exploit desperate migrants along their routes who wish to reach European soil. The migrant's risk everything to make that perilous journey with unworthy sea boats in order for their dream of a better life to be realized. The unscrupulous Libyan smugglers charge anywhere from 700 Euro to 3,000 Euro each for a person on the boat. However, the higher cost doesn't always translate into a better boat, as, as much as 420 persons could be crammed into a vessel meant to carry just a crew of seven. But as widely known in most cases, the vessels are unseaworthy and overstuffed. The smugglers barely provide enough fuel to make it to the international waters, and then abandon the boats, and their passengers to their fate. Most people are saved, thanks to the international navies, aid agencies, Frontex and commercial vessels. The mind-boggling question everyone including the aid agencies kept asking is, "why would people risks so much including their lives in order to reach Europe to achieve a better life that's often not guaranteed?" Especially when one from the very day he or she registers for asylum, might be hounded and troubled by the thoughts of deportation as the journey and slinging never stops, and so is their peace of mind even when one gets to Europe. But then again, when they remember the conditions lived by these desperate asylum seekers in their home countries including hunger, deprivation, lack of basic services, persecution, incessant clashes and crisis, some might just fathom, why they took the dreaded and lethal risks they took.

CHAPTER ONE

THE JOURNEY OF FRIENDS

It's 7 a. m. in the morning in April 2013 as the day broke. Osas woke up from his bed with the increasing impetuous and unbridled thoughts and notion of traveling to Europe to secure a brighter future, a place where almost all his friends and relatives have traveled to, in the last couple of years. Although, he's not sure if all of them have made it to Europe. Soaring and unrestrained thoughts that were constantly bogging him manifesting itself in a seething uneasiness even as he was at the curve of sitting for his secondary school final year exams and graduation. Like a state government official puts it, it's a cultural problem in this part of the country and common to have young men and women grow up with the adroit dream of a future that lie in the western world as they strive to overcome difficulties that lie on their way to travel abroad. By abroad, a familiar term loosely used in this country, they mean mostly Europe. "What about education?" What about getting a job back at home? "Settling down and having a family, getting old and dying in their land of birth?" It's a question everyone keeps asking themselves but it's obvious why. In a modern-day society where, young people envisage themselves being at the top of the world and their career shinning as they grow up only to come to the grip of reality that the economic situations facing their society might present an obstacle and may not allow such dreams to manifests. But as it presents rocky challenges, on one hand, it opens up another unorthodox door for exploration in order that they may reach their potentials or become the future as imagined. Now tell me why they would not explore the later.

It's actually the dream of every person not limited to the developing world to fully explore the boundaries of possibilities. However, this often occurs, when the economy is bad, not enough jobs are created to fill the increasing number of secondary and university graduates not just in this one popular town 'Benin city' but throughout the country and other parts of the continent. It's common to have people travel abroad by air but in this city most people believe they could actually travel abroad legally with or without official invitation from a relative or friend. After all, when the air travel is not possible, the land and road travel is readily available to explore for the numerous numbers of people seeking to get out of the country in search of a lustrous future or better life. But one would ask, "have they ever put into consideration all the risks the journey would present?" The possible violence, attacks, incessant extortion, bodily violation including rape of travelers at every leg and level of the journey, if one falls in the wrong hands especially the women even death. Also, trafficking and forced labour, the possible risk of being sold to slavery or used as a guinea pig for experiments as travelers body organs could be coercively harvested and sold to foreign buyers who pay a lot for the booming illicit trade across the Sahara. The list goes on and on of the perilous journey that takes a toll on its pilgrims seeking protection, freedom, a new beginning and the pursuit of happiness in a foreign land.

Osas was determined but he was seeking ways to see how possible it is to travel through to Europe by land. Not much thoughts are put on safety but how to get there and how long it takes to make the journey from Benin city to Libya and from that country's port through the sea to Europe. It's not new. It's a road that have been plied by many other thousands of young men and women not only from this city and country but across the West African region. News of its dangers have filled the air up until this time and the possible hardships, violence and forced labour, but what do you say or do to a determined person like Osas, whom even his mother can't stop because he uses the excuse of the journey of others who have successfully made it there to argue to travel over there, if he ever gets there. He went to have his hair shaved that morning and after wards asked his friend Simon, if his brother that traveled since the last two months have contacted him. "Yes, he did. From Libya. He arrived safely," replied Simon to him. But the journey was tough, strenuous especially to and from Agadez along the Sahara Desert. He is there waiting for the right time, an opportunity to present itself with a boat to be able to journey across. "But it's not easy, right? Many have thought of spending one or two months there only to end up staying in Libya for five years or more, right?" Osas flickering and shrugging asked him. That's life. It's either your makeup your mind to go or not go. Not all have the same luck", his friend Simon responding added. The hair shaving came to a finish. He looks himself in the mirror, Hmmm, cute haircut, said Osas. You're welcome, answered Simon. He then left back home.

He began to make other contacts around and among his family and friends, gathering facts and gaining knowledge, especially from the ones who have traveled before, and things didn't turn out well, and were either deported or established their businesses back home and decided to come back home with their families. It's going to be a learning curve for Osas, for the next coming months as he prepares to leave his motherland to an unknown and uninsured path into a journey he doesn't know how it will end up. But that's just the first step as the second step of preparation was to seek out those who could lend him money to enable him to travel. He has been asking his mum for a long time to sell a certain piece of land handed to them by their grand father in order to raise money. But for over a year his mother has tried to skew him off those thoughts and let him know the importance of that land being there as insurance, in case he travels abroad and succeeds or any of his siblings succeeds in life, they could build their house on that land. He has failed to convince his mother, even with the promises he makes to his mother of succeeding in Europe. His mother may have had experience in that field too or heard stories of people who ended up not making it to Europe. Either they are killed on the way, drowned in the Mediterranean Sea or are jailed in a far away land for crime. So, she didn't want to take that risk and she was not standing on the way of her son either.

Her husband and father of Osas passed away recently from heart surgery. The family is barely coming to terms with their father's passing, as all still seems fresh in his mother's eyes as she's sometimes overcome with grief. But on the other hand, that's simply a stimulator for Osas. As the first born, though young, he is beginning to see himself as the breadwinner. But not yet as he must first finish his secondary school that year. But he's under pressure now that his father has passed away. The question is, why are his first driving thoughts, that of traveling to Europe and not trying to get a job or training locally in order to make ends meet after his secondary education. The answer is simple, there are no jobs. Secondly, a country whose leaders have been the cause of the suffering their people are in, in spite of the huge resources developed to enable the country cope with its enormous challenges, how could the same leaders, still recycled in power, have changed even after decades have passed, as if they've not learned anything. Tell me how the government could think of something so noble for its people to help curb the issue of incessant youth restiveness, crime and above all, the travels beyond the border and risks associated with them. Getting educational training whether in schools including vocational practical training requires money, energy and time to train such a person until the person gets better at a profession. But those vocational programs, though, by far the most effective way to tackle the issues of poverty and economic migration have been lacking in the public educational system neither are the people-oriented policies to advocate for such social reforms. If only they were seen as viable, formulated and implemented, it could've helped many and avoided the issues we have or are facing in the country, and other places in Africa, Middle East and in Europe right now. Not least, those within the country who've lost hope in the government and resort to social vices such as armed robbery, kidnapping or thefts, being bedeviled with no form of education and opportunities.

Osas is the more determined to travel and he needs money. He believes when there's money, the path and understanding to getting to Libya and then Europe will open up or become clearer. He knew someone who knows a ruthless gang that are notorious in armed robbery involving banks and business locations even breaking into private homes to raid. He had made his inquiries about them. "Would he join them?" But first he must ask his friend to connect him to them. When he summoned up courage and did, his friend told him, "It's a dangerous game, and when you are caught, your dream of traveling abroad may be dashed. Go and think about it because once you start, you may not want to travel again especially if it pays off really good". Once again go and think about it, said his friend to him. "No, I don't have to think about it. I need money to pay for my journey. I believe in just once. If they allow me to be a part of them, after one successful operation, I'm out" said Osas to his friend. Okay. The head of the gang is my brother. Give me two days to get in contact with them, if you are lucky and they want you. Then, I'll call for you. If not, then, look somewhere else for money, okay? Agreed, answered Osas

After two days, his friend Igbinidion called his phone line. "Hello," Said Igbinidion. "Yes," hello, answered Osas. "Come tomorrow and I will take you to them. They have agreed to meet with you," said his friend to him. "Elated, I'll be there tomorrow," replied Osas. The next day he was all ready and went over to his friend, who then took him to meet this secretive but fierce group of night raiders called "The Eagle Eye." Reaching there, he met Black Arrow, its commander, who asked him, "Are you prepared to do this?"

Your friend told me you want to travel abroad, and you need money to pay for your fare?" Yes, answered Osas. Why didn't you just go to the motor-park? There are plenty of petty jobs you could do there even as a bus conductor, after a couple of months or years, you could get the money you seek to travel abroad?" No, he replied.

It's a very tedious work. Secondly, it could take a long time to gather the money I need while they are people around who constantly need money to sort out their issues. Okay, since you've made up your mind. Then I ask, go and come back tomorrow and you'll meet other members of this group. But I warn you, when once you're inside, it's very tempting and it's hard to get out. That also means you suspending your trip abroad even in the near future. If we succeed, the mouth-watering reward you get from that operation, will make sure of that," He added.

On the next day and at the exact time, he made himself available at the exact venue as he was called into a room, inside he met astonishing people with faces, some of which were familiar to him. He was introduced to the group by their leader. Osas, standing before you here want to be part of us and we have decided to let him, Arrow, introduced him to them. He wants to travel abroad, to Europe but needs money to make that journey that's why he wants to do this," said their leader to the group. "I've warned him that it's hard to get inside but getting out is even harder." However, he insisted of being part of us until he gets what he wants. Ladies and gentle men, I introduce to you, Osas Erebuwa." Every member of the group present there clapped and shook his hand welcoming him in. He sat down and exchanged pleasantries with all the people he knew including his niece.

"Evelyn, you are part of them too?" I couldn't have imagined" Said he to his niece. "Life is unfair. It has thrusted me into this shit. Just like you want to travel abroad to go and earn a good living. I'm trying to make mine here, doing this..." she replied to him. The process is not yet finished, said Black Arrow to him. Before we drill you on how things roll here, we'll first of all, take you to the chief wizard, the Juju priest, to carry out a ritual on you to get you fortified. An insurance spells. "The second aspect of the ritual is for you to swear an allegiance to this group, never to betray us. If you ever do, you will die, by the nature of the rituals used against you," Said Black Arrow to him. He paused and looked at them as they gazed at him. "What's your response?", "What say you, brother" Asked Black Arrow. Reluctantly, "okay," answered Osas to them. "But what does it entail?" Asked Osas. Not much. Just swear to this and that, especially not betraying or revealing our identity to the police or anyone outside those already aware. If you did, then, the Juju would vent an angry vengeance against you for not keeping to the terms of the secret pact.

"Believe me, it's serious business." We are not joking here, said Black Arrow, head of the group to him. Moreover, 'never play with the sacred rites of Juju, it's dangerous.' Everyone gazing at him still, expecting an answer. I came here because I need help from you guys, to be part of your group for one hit only. When it's successful, I earn my dough. I'll quit and use the money to make my journey abroad but if I must do this, then, it's okay. Everyone hailed and celebrated him and his bold decision. You can relax now. In the evening, by 7p.m., we'll go over to the Juju priest to carry out these rituals of swearing and joining you to this group. They drank and celebrated and in the evening at the exact hour they had planned, they then set out to go over to the place of the Juju priest, who was already informed and waiting for them to arrive.

By the way, the Juju priest's shrine was an extension of his private residence. This Juju or voodoo priest like all other practitioners of the Earth religion, in this region of the country earn their living from carrying out these kinds of divination hoodoo rituals that tie people to a dark magical curse, if clients are interested in invoking a contract pact with divination ritual. Something that goes beyond the realm of understanding of common criminals to smugglers who patronize them by bringing many of such quick fortune seeking people ranging from young men and women who are desperate to get rich quick through Internet scams or travel abroad in search of a good life. It's reported that the Juju priests earn much more from the Internet fee fraudsters. I always wonder why this old mean phony guys not arrested for misleading their desperate clients.

On this nightfall, they arrived. Though reluctant, because his family were Christians and would naturally not do such a thing but so are all others, as this was a Christian state in the south of the country, but he was determined to get out of Nigeria, and nothing could stand on his way to achieving his aim, no matter the consequences which were often overwhelming and feared by initiates of such a scam ritual but nonetheless a dangerous ancient traditional religious initiation rites meted on innocent young men and women. And although, Osas had heard of the devilry and Djinn jinx hunting spells associated with this black art rituals told him by other travelers who were smuggled across the desert, one would think, this might give him a pause to think, or, his path might be different since he was working hard to pay for his fares and cover many other unforeseen expenses, but we'll later realize that no one is free willed in this treachery and mumbo jumbo game of smugglers across the Saharan territories whether it's in your interest or not. But first things first, and that were the mystical initiations into a rite to belong to a criminal gang that earn a living on meting pain, sorrow and suffering to other innocent members of the public. The very ones that the nation's economic policies suppress and who live day to day trying to make a good life for their families. Not long after they'd arrived had the initiation started as the chief priest asked Osas, "I was told you want to be part of this gang and that you have accepted to adhere to their number one rule, which was the rule of initiation into the unbreakable bond between the members of this group where you under no circumstances are allowed to betray any member of this group and any day you do so, even when you are arrested by the police and under oath, you'll die?" Said the Juju priest to him. "Die?" Is that not too extreme a curse for joining an armed robbery group?"

Those are the conditions, said Black Arrow to him. Looking at them, once again, 'okay,' He replied. I agree. Alright, let's do this, he responded. The next step is to begin the ritual on your body, said the high priest. This ritual I'm about to carry out would do two things to you. First, it will protect you against the eyes and weapons of your enemies that seek your fall, making you impregnable and helping you to evade the plans, detection and arrest by the Police. Secondly, it ties you to the bond of this group and as long as you're loyal to them, you have nothing to fear. But any day, you betray this group, this curse ritual will hunt and kill you immediately. "I'm I clear enough?",

"Okay?" Asked the Juju priest. "Okay," replied Osas. The Juju priest holding fresh leaf on his hand, asked, Osas to remove his shirt. He did immediately, as he used the fresh conditioned mystery leaf to perform a cleansing ritual on him while chanting to the Gods of the Earth. After which, he used a native sea chalk to write some certain signs on his back, shoulders and chest while chanting continually under a mysterious smoke that fills the shrine. It was a ritual that took about an hour and lastly after some precise magic cuts to the body, some back of baobab tree cooked in a fire was given him to chew for ten minutes. Surrounding him several times, asked him, to say yes to anything he, the Juju priest says. He bowed in agreement as he did the same as required by the Juju priest. After which, the Juju priest told him stand up, for the initiation rituals are over. He did so, groaning and squeaking after kneeling for a long time. The Juju priest told him, from now you're protected from the prying eyes of your enemies, and you'll succeed in your goals. Secondly, "I repeat again, in case you didn't hear me very well, the very day you betray or reveal the identity of any member of your group to the police under any circumstances, that day you shall die." You should know that. "I will not," he replied. Even, if you succeed in traveling abroad, you have no right over there to tell anyone about the activities of this gang. "Okay?" Asked the Juju priest to him.

"Okay," once again, replied him to them. You may now go, said the Juju priest to them.

Black Arrow embraced him along with other members of his new criminal gang, as the head of the group brought out a bundle of money from his pocket and gave to the Juju priest for his services that night. It's hectic, said Black Arrow to him. "It's my work. Anytime," replied the Juju priest back to him. They then left. That night reaching back to their hired apartment, where they all gather. A separate apartment he rented in the town for their meeting. Do you want to stay with us for the night or return home to your family, Arrow asked. I will like to go home. My mum will be looking for me already. Remember, never tell anyone about this, including your Mum, okay?

Black arrow added to him. "Okay," he replied. I will not tell anyone. He then left back home. Reaching home, already too late his mother worried about him asked, "Osas, where have you been?" I have called your phone line several times but no reply. I thought something bad had happened to you. Nothing, Mum. I'm fine. Said Osas to his mother. Okay, go to the kitchen. Your food is there. It must be already cold. But you could warm it. Okay, thanks Mum. He went to the kitchen and accessed his food, warmed it and ate. Afterwards, feeling sleepy, he went to bed to sleep. The next day, in the morning, he left to meet with his new group, telling his mother, he's gone to see a friend concerning his plans of traveling abroad and to see, if the father of his friend could borrow him money to use and travel abroad. "Even, if I have to work for him, I will, just to make sure the money is sufficient enough to help me make my trip abroad." Be careful, Son. "Don't be desperate to do what will come back to bite you," retorted her mother to him. If I could help, I would have done so. I'm only a food stuff retailer in the market. All I have is that which is enough to feed this family. Nothing more, added the mother. No problem, responded Osas to his mother.

He left and arrived at the point where they all meet for a meeting to plan on their next target. He was then drilled on what it takes. The apartment big enough was used as a simulation ground for their next planned target. After an hour, Black arrow told him, our next target is to attack a businessman, who just arrived from Lagos. I was reliably told by an employee of the bank that this man would be withdrawing up to ten million naira to pay the contractor who was handling a building construction, a contract he got from a consortium which intend to build a finance institution in Benin city. We'll be paid equally when we succeed along with our informer at the bank. Your cut can enable you to make your journey. It will be enough, right? Yes. In calculation, it's more than enough, responded Osas to him. You see, I told you. If we start and you see the gains, you might even abandon your plans of traveling abroad, said Black Arrow to him. They all laughed. They whole thing will be going down in five days time. We have three days to drill you in live gun shooting. By tomorrow, we'll take you to Abama bush, A simulation ground. There, we'll practice the live shots firing, added Black Arrow. After their meeting, he left. He got home early. Excited of the prospects, and the lustrous promise of the money they could earn if all goes according to plan. But in these kinds of gangs, though not all, they hardly recount the consequences of failure. They expect you to know that. Because those gangs who have failed have languished many years in jail. Others shot right away by the Police, who don't live to tell the tales.

The next day at the time, they promised to meet. They met and got a car and traveled a few kilometers outside the town. A place they'll be doing their practice on how to counter an attack in the event of any unforeseen resistance by the law enforcement agencies. They entered and rode to the Abama bush, a place they were conversant with. A place that they regularly use for their training. Soon had they arrived has their training effectively started as they spent a couple of hours simulating on how he could handle a loaded gun and to shoot without fear. Also, how they could do it in a uniformed fashion, so that in the end, in the event of such feared situation happening they could manage to return safe. After three hours, they entered back into their car and returned. The experience was exhilarating as it was frightful. But the next two days of training might cement the experience and make him more comfortable even as they prepare to attack a target. That day soon came as they were all prepared. In the apartment. The night before, Black Arrow told him, usually this situation does not involve shooting. As all we have to do is to trail the victim and follow him to the point outside the bank where he intends to drop off the bag of money and then we'll come out and surround him, get the money quickly and then, without hurting anyone drive away. It's simple. But it could go worse. That is, when the money bearer is aware of the plan and had informed the Police, then things could get out of hands. Also, sometimes, a civilian might want to act as a hero and such person might get hurt. These are the minor set backs. Otherwise, we are good and we could do this. It's not a big deal. "Are you ready for this?" Asked Black Arrow to Osas. Yes, I think so. "Are you ready?" Asked him again. "Yes," I am. Okay, good. That's the kind of spirit I want you to inculcate. Don't be weak. "Don't breakdown even in the face of a fierce attack, Okay?" Said Black Arrow. Okay, answered back Osas.

With the correct information received of the target and where he would be withdrawing his money from and the number of security guards guarding the bank and the possible place he might be heading afterwards, they felt ready. "Go home, rest and get prepared." To-morrow at 1pm, we'll move. The whole thing will go down at about 3pm tomorrow just before the banks close up. We'll get there early and wait. The Bank informer will call us immediately the target individual enters the bank and confirmed to be the one. "Okay?" replied Osas. Tomorrow by 1pm, I will be here, answered Osas. Good, replied Black Arrow. He went home that night. But he couldn't sleep. The anxiety and unrelenting ruffled perturbation. He was troubled that night. He swung from left to right of his bed in distressing antic-ipation of what was going to happen. In the morning, the continuous rattling thoughts unnerved him. His stroking body and fazed mind apparently jolting and his eyes reddish, his mother during breakfast asked, what's the matter? Is anything the matter? Nothing Mummy. I'm fine, answered Osas back to his mother. Obviously, he didn't look okay. That's why his mother asked the question. I've told you severally, don't allow desperation to put us into trouble. Are you ow-ing anyone anything or done something terrible? No, nothing. I'm fine. After the meal, the mother went into the room to pray, believing all was not well with his son. She suspected that his drive to travel abroad must have taken him to the wrong people. Though she was not sure, what people were those. But in her heart, she was thinking something terrible might happen to her son. She came out of the room and told his son, 'come with me.' He came to her. They went outside to the corner of their house. She pointed to the grave of his father buried close to their house, saying look at your father, dead and buried there. "Do you want his death to be in vain?" I don't know, what you are up to now, because you're not telling me anything about yourself and your activities, since you finished secondary school education. But make sure, we don't lose you for nothing, all because you seek money to travel to Europe. You could still survive even if you live in this country. Mummy, I told you it's nothing, Said Osas to his mother. I hope so. I hope what you're telling me, is true.

They then went into the house together as she told them, I'm off to the market. Take care of yourselves, after preparing her younger children for school. Immediately, his mother left for her business in the market, he quickly prepared to meet the other members of his new group. An hour later, they entered their vehicle and left to the area of the bank where the cash withdrawals will be made by their target victim about to be attacked. They arrived and as usual they waited. While waiting they had assumed any of the people entering the bank could be the target. But it was at exactly 3:20 pm that a call came in telling them, "Get prepared", as the informer described the man and the dressing he wore that day to them so as for them to identify him, when he comes out with the money. They were told in ten minutes, he should be through with the transaction and will come out of the bank, then follow him. Black Arrow echoed, copy. We'll do exactly so. Just at the exact time, they were told. They prepared and ignited the car. They drove forward closer to the bank in order to identify the target when he gets out.

At the exact time, they were told, appeared the target with the right clothing he was described to wear. He came down the stairs, with his briefcase filled with ten million Naira. Entered into his brand-new Toyota car and drove off. They have confirmed him to be the one, they followed.

They drove for about twenty minutes. Then, reaching the destination of the building construction, the target drove his car into the compound of the construction. Then, they behind, stopped their car outside the building and entered immediately. Just as the construction site gate was about to close. They stormed inside with their guns and rifles ready to attack. They surrounding the car ordered him out of the car. He slowly did with one hand up and the other handling the suitcase. One of them, immediately collected the suitcase from him. With a shout, let's go. Meant they were now finished there and were ready to move out. They were many people in the construction site who also witnessed the event, but they all took cover at the instructions of the armed robbers who ordered all of them to go down or be shot. They all obeyed. Black Arrow collected the money bag and brought it back to the target to open it for him to confirm if it was money. 'Open it,' he shouted at the business contractor. The target opened it up and all he saw was money. He closed it up quickly and with his people they fled the site. Outside, they entered their car and left. But before they left, they made sure they disarmed everyone of the workers, by collecting all their mobile phones away from them. By doing so, they made sure, they could successfully flee that area before anyone got a phone to call the police to come and intervene in the situation. They fled successfully.

But like most armed robbers in this country, they didn't cover their faces as they robbed all not fearing retribution, that someone might identify them and describe them to the police. They had done that severally especially after doing their home work knowing it's of no consequence as they could hardly be detected. With no surveillance camera showing solid evidence such case might be eventually thrown out of the court. They were daring in their act. This was a robbery that had went on smoothly without anyone getting hurt or anyone dying. To the new recruit, Osas, he was particularly happy that they succeeded without him having a breakdown. They all reached home and were happy that they successfully carried out this operation. "It could have been worse," Black Arrow told Osas. In this business anything can happen at anytime. After celebration that night, they brought out the money and shared it equally. Black arrow counted 1.6 Million Naira and gave to Osas. Osas couldn't believe his eyes. "Do you still wanna travel to Europe?" He asked Osas, while others laughed around. Being quiet for sometimes, said yes, I still want to travel abroad. This traveling to Europe. Everybody going to Europe. "What do you think is in Europe, anyways?"

"Nothing." I've been there and back, said Black Arrow. It's on history that every house in this city must have at least one person in Europe who traveled in search of greener pastures. They all know that, you don't get rich traveling to Europe. But is better than staying in their country. Many especially the women who travel to countries such as Italy end up in prostitution rings in order to feed themselves and their families back home. Most times, they do so as trafficked victims.

He got his money and liked the smell of it. Excited that his journey might begin in earnest. He was also sure, having made up his mind that he might not go for another hit or operation of robbery since he has now got everything he wanted. Where are you taking this money to? Asked his niece. Take it home and hide it. Then tomorrow, try and open an account in the Bank and put some of this money inside the account, Okay? Okay, I'll do that, answered Osas. They drank some more wine and alcohol, which he didn't participate, and after wards he left. He sneaked the money into his room and hid it. That night he couldn't sleep. This time anxious, may be someone among his friends could set him up and come to take away his money that night. He thought the money in the room was not safe. He eventually slept and the next day. They ate some food, as he told his mother. Mummy, I now got the money to travel to Europe? 'Really?" Who gave it to you? And what are you going to do to pay back the money? Asked his Mother. Nothing. I told you about the father of my friend. I told him, of my plight, about my plans to travel out while working part-time in his company. He called me yesterday and gave me the money. "How much" Asked the mother? 200,000 Naira. That is so much money. "What did you do to deserve that much money?" I hope, you didn't commit a sexual act with the man for money. I hear a lot of young boys are into homosexual acts with rich people, these days, to earn a good living. Any day, I hear you do that, I'll kill you myself. No, Mummy. It's none of that. Good, answered the mother.

After the mother went to her business that morning, he took out some money and went to the bank to open and deposit in a savings account. Knowing fully well of the law of the federal government of Nigeria not depositing too much money into the account in excess of 500,000 Naira, if not, one will attract the eyes of the financial crimes commission. Who would want to know what he does to earn such a large amount of money. He deposited 500,000 Naira in the bank. Just the limit of cash an individual is not expected to exceed. He was glad. After wards, he went to join the group that evening to tell them, he was now ready to make his journey and that he wanted out. When they gathered, he told them, I've got all I want. I want to quit the group and prepare for my Journey.

"When is your journey," asked Black Arrow. Don't know exactly. Maybe in two to three weeks. That is still enough time to support us launch another targeted attack. "Can you?" Asked Black Arrow. "No, I can't," replied Osas. It's not a question, said Arrow. We helped you. Now we want your help one last time. His niece cut in to say, let him go. Cut him loose. No, dear. We need his help one more time, before he can be free from us to go wherever he wants to go, added Black Arrow. "Can you perform one more operation?" asked her niece. I don't know. But I told you all that I will quit when I get the money I need. I think I got all I want. I don't want to be part of your activities anymore, said Osas. We are not arguing here. It's either you do as you're told, or I'll inform the Juju priest that you have broken the bond contract. You know, there is punishment prescribed for breaking such promises, Arrow leaning forward, threatened. In this part of the country, the fear of Juju or voodoo, is the beginning of wisdom. That is because they know what Juju can do to one far outstrips the threats or punishment of any other enemy including the Police. It's simply, feared. But the question is, if it's so much feared, why do almost every one here engage in it, in doing everything they do in their personal and business life knowing the consequences of failing to meet its demand. While, it's forced on some who mostly want to travel outside the country by their smugglers, others see it as a source of protection or fortification against an enemy.

Right there, not wanting any retribution from the angry Gods, he agreed. Good, now we understand ourselves very well. After this, you can go. I promise, you'll be fine. Nothing will happen to you. Just as it happened the last time. The operation I believe would go on smoothly. Although not convinced of what Black Arrow was saying, having heard lots of tales of the last operation, being the one that breaks the camels back or injures the offender, he was the more worried. Don't worry, it will be okay. Nothing would happen to you, I promise, said his niece to him. "Are you sure of that?" Asked Osas. Yeah, I'm sure. You'll be fine, she tapped him at the back and smiled.

"What kind of operation and when would that be," Osas further asked. In two weeks, give or take, just the exact time you need to prepare for your journey. But after this, you're free to leave or travel out, whatever you want to do. You will get more money, I promise you. Come tomorrow and we will brief you on this operation, added Black Arrow to him. He went home confused and troubled.

Should I run away? He thought to himself. Or, "should I still join them for this one last operation." What if after this one, Arrow again says, one more? What if this one is much more dangerous than the last one and someone probably gets killed in the process? All these were the questions he kept unloading on himself.

Eventually, he slept and the next day as usual he reported at the place where they meet to organize their robbery operations. A Nigerian business man resident in America is landing here in one- or two-week's time. We'll confirm from his unsuspecting relative, once he arrives. He will be coming with lots of money to use and start a business or build a house, or whatever they said he wants to do when he gets back. But what's important is that, he'll come with lots of money in Dollars, the excited gang all screamed. We want that money. So, when he arrives, before he begins to spend that money we'll pay him a visit. I mean, we'll attack his home. His home? Asked Osas. Yes, his home and we will take the money.

He then trained him as they aligned their training to ensure when the time comes it was executed without mistakes. He was drilled on what he should do when they get in. "You will ensure the family stays down with their faces covered on the ground and their phone handsets collected away from them. The security man will be tied up and taken along. When the house is secured, and compound cleared, we will bring the necessary equipment to ensure the iron doors or windows are sawed opened," Black Arrow laid out the plan. What is he in America? Asked Osas. He is a business man and an investment banker in one of the top banking firms in America. I heard he's the chief executive of the American Bank. I don't know which one. All I know, is that he is rich. He might not feel the money because he has much more. He has a duplex house in the city's housing estate and that is where he might stay when he arrives. So, they all prepared towards this day. They knew how the house looks like and the protective proof used to secure the doors and windows and they were sure they will tear them safely down to enter inside the house, with the right equipment when that day comes. After all, it's not their first time doing this. At most they'll use an explosive to tear the door apart or tear through the wall by boring a round hole through the house walls to get inside to carry out their operation.

Either ways, based on their experience they were sure to successfully carry out this hit. The time came, and it was reported that the target victim was already in the country. Like they planned, that day should not pass, his residence must be attacked. If not, more time, will leave room for him disposing off, the money he brought with him, from the United States. So, having confirmed that he arrived Benin city on this day. That night they departed for their operation. Reaching there, as planned. They stormed through the outside gate, apprehended the security man and tied him up. Then, moved him forward to the house which doors were well secured and locked. But they must break in, no matter how impregnable it might look. They brought out their equipment and began sawing away the iron proof off the window after they had removed the mosquito nets protection and the window sliding glasses. It took them time to saw through the iron protectors, which time, a member of the family who was not asleep at about 2 a.m., but watching a movie noticed something was wrong. He came down through the stairs only to see that they were near completing the sawing of the iron protectors. He then shouted. Immediately, he did that the whole house woke up as they called the police immediately to come around to help counter the armed robbery in progress.

But soon, were they done, they pushed themselves through the windows inside the house as they immediately went to and knocking down every room to bring out everyone. Then, finally the master bed room to get their target. They collected all their smart phones. Without wasting time. Arrow ordered their foreign target to take them to his room, where he kept all the money. If he didn't produce all the money, he will be killed, they threatened him. They walked through the stairs back to his room as he opened his briefcase and brought out all the money he had on him. Fortunately, for him, he changed some of the Dollars into the local exchange currency and put some in the bank on the first day as if he knew what he was doing. But the bulk of the foreign currency laid in the house and that was all he brought out totaling 30,000 Dollars. Traveling internationally, one is not allowed to carry that much money. This means he withdrew much of that money from his local foreign currency account. Perhaps, to be used for an urgent local business project. They collected them but walked with him down as he joined the rest in the living room. The Police came but it was too late. It took the Police an hour to respond but they were done in less than forty minutes and left the scene.

The Police arrived but saw terrified and traumatized victims of horrible armed robbery and abuse crying and wailing on the floor. Why did you come late? Asked the victims. We had to fill the fuel tank first and prepare. You know, these were armed robbers. If we came unprepared, some of us could get killed including you too. That was what happened, responded the police officer. Well, you arrived late, and they are long gone, said the target victim. We'll investigate. Don't worry, we'll find the culprits, apprehend them and prosecute them for their crime, said the Police officer.

Of course, it's the Police everyone knew. What will they say? That is the same B.S., they do and say every time. "Why should the people need to rely on an unreliable Police force, when they are not always there when needed to protect the people, the civil populace, the reason, for which the institution was set up?" While the Police were busy floundering with their inadequacies and lack of competency, the thieves were terrorizing their target and were now long gone. If they were well equipped by the government with Biometric, fingerprint, scan, tracking and other body features recognition and analyzing technology, their investigation might be sped off and culprits caught immediately. But that might be possible if that country has a data bank of all its citizens. But I bet you, Nigeria doesn't know all its citizens. That's why they keep giving contradictory estimate of the country's population. Today, its 170 million people. Tomorrow it's 200 million people. Some people don't believe in those figures they give because more and more people in Nigeria today do family planning. Even, those in the villages or smaller towns, after the third child, they begin to ask questions. Because their income can't feed all the mouths neither afford their education as the children grow up. In times past, fathers could marry three or more wives but today many Nigerian men marry just one wife with the number of kids they could afford to take care of. Secondly, a country that doesn't offer free universal health care to its people as more people rely on traditional institutions and religious houses to give birth and get cured when sick. How is it possible for the country to gather the data needed to know who a Nigerian is truly and who's not.

Well, successful at the second hit without being caught, especially for the first timer, Osas, it was a big deal for him. This means he has personally witnessed death and has twice survived it. That is because increasingly, there are reported cases of how several bandits groups are being caught monthly. As part of this work, every time you carryout an operation and it worked out well, then, it's a thing to rejoice about since not all are that lucky. This means with the risk of being found out as investigation rolls on this case at hand, it reinforces the desire for this teenager to want to eagerly make the journey he has always hoped to make.

In their operation base, they all uncladed themselves, as Osas went to a corner to pray to God, saying the words; Thank you God for saving me, I promise not to do it again. While doing that, others watching him laughed, as one said, come here and sit down. No problem. You don't have to worry, you're safe. I have been doing this for many years, even before joining this group. The chance of the Police catching us is slim not unless there's a surveillance camera somewhere recording the event, or we are leaving traces behind. But even in that, they don't have Biometric finger-print and DNA technology at the Police department. That means the probability of we are being caught in leaving traces of evidence is low or non-existent. Secondly, non of those people recognized us. Once again, in clarity of the situation, you are safe. You can walk out here boldly without anyone recognizing you or knowing that you did something wrong while you enjoy your money. But make sure while anyone of you spend your money, you are moderate, so that you don't attract unnecessary attention or eyebrows, Okay? Said one of the bandits. It's late, relax and sleep. Tomorrow, you could go home. I know your mother would be worried about you, but you could find any excuse and tell her, Okay? It's already 3 a.m., said his niece to him. I already told my younger one to tell my mother I will not be home for the night. That I'll be with a friend for the night, responded Osas to the rest of them. That's good, said Black Arrow. They all relaxed, some were awake and watched TV, while others slept.

The next morning Osas, was given his cut. His share of the loot which was 6,000 dollars. That was so much money for him. It was more money than he earned from their last hit. Now, he is worth about Four Million Naira. With that money, in 2013, one can build a small house in Benin city and hire it out. Then, collect rent on yearly basis. A situation that might ensure he's never poor again even if he lives in Nigeria. But for a teenager, that will definitely raise eyebrows. And nothing is hidden in this town as rumours easily spread. When it does, it could attract both good and bad including the Police to his doorstep unexpectedly. Once again, the thought of traveling to Europe is ringing in his ears. Before he left that morning, his niece, shouted at Black Arrow saying, free him; free him now. In front of everyone, Black arrow said to him, having served your cause in this group faithfully though with fear and not breaking the rules of this group and with the promise of not breaking it in future, we now free you from this group to pursue your goals of traveling to Europe. He was ecstatic. They all embraced him as they warned him once again, never, never, not here, not there in Europe, think of ever opening your mouth to let people into our secret, Okay? I promise with all my heart. I will never tell anyone, promised Osas to the group he'll be separating from.

"Do we need to go to the Juju priest to break the curse?" Asked Osas. After a momentary silence, said his niece to him, when you're prepared to travel to Libya, we'll go there to break the spell from you while casting another on you for protection. You know, you have to perform the ritual of protection. Everybody does it. Anyone who plans to travel abroad does it to fortify his or herself against abuse, death, failure and disappointment and most of all to curry favour from those who'll receive him or her at the other end. You know what I mean? Added his niece. Yes, I understand. I have been told that I must carryout that rituals before I depart for Libya because a lot of bad things take place on the road leading to Libya not to mention the deaths on the way. I need favour from the Gods. We all need protection, replied Osas to all of them as he left for home with his own share of the money well secured in his inner pant pockets. He didn't want to leave any room for error, in case one comes to snatch the money away suspecting that someone out there must be aware of what they did or on the other hand, risk his mother searching his pockets in suspicion when he arrives home.

Reaching home, his mother asked him, "Boy, where have you been the whole night?" I was with my friend Onome. "But I told John to inform you that I may not be returning. That I might sleep at their house," said Osas to his mother. "And why should you do that?" Don't you have a home? You want people to call us names? By the way, tell me again, what you did for that man to give you all that money to cover your traveling expenses? "Are you sure, you didn't tell me lies but did something else to get that money?" inquired the mother again. No, Mummy, I've told you already as he left her presence to his room. Go and get your food and make sure you put that money in the bank until you're ready to travel abroad, Okay? Shouted the mother as he entered and bounced his room door behind him to a close. Okay, Mum. I'll do that. Stay home and take care of your young ones, I am going to the market to attend to my customers, Okay? Said the mother as she stood outside his room door. Okay, Mum? Replied Osas. Immediately, the mother left for the market stall, Osas came out of his room. He told John, his junior brother, look here, I'll be back soon. Take care of your little brother. Before you close your eyes and open them, I'm back. I'll buy some snacks for you guys, okay? Said Osas to his junior brother. "Okay," replied his junior brother to him. He immediately left to the city centre, a district where they are many foreign currencies exchange booths, to exchange the dollars into Naira, the local currency used in Nigeria. Reaching there, he exchanged in equivalent of 500,000 Naira, the exact money allowed for an individual deposit at any given time. Once again, he went to the bank and saved the money in his account. In the coming days, he'll ensure up to two Million Naira from the money he stole was deposited in the bank.

During that period, he was also busy making inquiries and finalizing his attempts at resolving all the necessary things he needed in order to travel out of Benin to Kano city, the city that would lead him eventually across the border into Niger Republic, the neighbouring country at the northern axis. But not yet as he must first carry out that legendary traditional ceremony of protection from the Juju priest. So, a day was set along with other members of his former gang as they went to then Juju priest to perform the rituals of breaking the spell upon him while performing another of blessing upon him. It seems complicated but it's actually not but we'll soon know what it all entails. Reaching there on this planned date alongside his crew, he met another girl waiting outside the Baba's shrine. "Hello! What's your name?" Asked Osas. "I am Nene," replied the girl. "What did you come here to do?" He asked the young lady. You know, the deal. You should already have guessed why I'm here. But the question from me is, is that not the same reason why you came to see Baba too? I guess in the affirmative, yes, replied Osas. "Maybe we can travel together. Is that possible?" By the way, when are you traveling? Asked Osas? In three days, from today, answered the young lady. Soon towering over them, was the presence of Baba, as he called in the Bandit gang. Young lady, I'll attend to you after them. They booked for this session earlier than you, Okay? Asked Baba. But I was here before them, replied the young lady. Like I said, don't worry, I'll attend to you immediately I'm done with them, Okay? Alright, I've heard you. I'll wait, answered the young lady.

Inside, they shook hands with Baba. "So, I heard you are done with the group, and are prepared to now travel abroad?" Asked Baba to Osas. Yes, Baba, replied the young man. Okay, sit down. Like you know, there's nothing the ancestral 'Gods' can't do. When we come to them in prayers and request, they are sure to always heed our requests, only when you abide by their instructions and don 't flout them. Now, we'll not do everything, we did the last time but nonetheless, when we are finished here, you should know that you're free from the curse of the bond, Okay? Asked Baba. Okay, replied Osas. Kneel here, he asked Osas. Osas came forward and knelt down as he carried out the rituals on him by starting with living mystery leaf to cleanse him. Then, rolled another leaf onto him and with smoke he exhaled the rolled-out leaf enchanted smoke into his two ears and mouth. Afterwards, asking him to remove his shirt, he then, drew some signs on his body with the local white sea chalk. He danced around him several times with traditional chants and then asked him to repeat after him. "From this day, as I promised not to break the rules of my former group and did the same as sworn, and now I have officially left the group and wished to be freed of the spell associated with the rituals cast on me, and right now, that curse is lifted off me. I am free from this group from any rules or strings that once tied us together." He repeated just exactly as the Juju priest said. Afterwards, the Juju priest raised him up and shaking his hand, said to him, 'you're free.' Now we'll carry out the second rituals of protection. He asked him once again to kneel, as he knelt down, and the mystery craft was applied with detailed steps of ancient traditional rites used long ago.

It was the same African mystery art used during the Trans Atlantic slave trade to protect men, women and children from being sold or abducted on the way while putting chains on them and forcing them into ships to be transported to the Americas. But during this mystical hoodoo ritual all other gang members must leave the shrine and go out since it has nothing to do with them. It's taught that this part contains a dark art involving body lacerations and spilling blood of a rare creature. After he was done, a process that took about twenty minutes, he finally stood up. He opened his pockets and brought out the exact amount asked for by the Juju priest to pay him for his services. "Go, you don't have any problem, you're fortified, and you'll soar over your enemies and your rivals," added the Juju priest to him.

He then went outside and met the rest of his former crew. But before the young lady went inside he quickly asked her, "Please could you give me your number?" I will call or write you. So that we could make the journey together. Together is better than alone into the unknown, He said to her. Yes, you are right. I'd love to, as they exchanged numbers in order to be in communication with one another in the coming days. Soon, came the Baba outside to call the young lady inside. The bandit crew greeted him goodbye as he did the same to them … Goodbye, my children. May Osalobua be with you. "Osalobua" being the name of God. Of course, one should expect even the

Juju priest to call on the name of the sky God, being that according to survey, most people in this state devote equally to both the worship of Juju Gods and the Christian God. They have no problem combining the two faiths in order to lead a healthy cultural and safe daily life. They all left while the lady came inside the shrine to be attended to by the Juju priest. But her kind of rituals would be different as she was being trafficked. Like I said, everyone whether one likes it or not, consciously or not, everyone will soon find out that before the journey ends he or she is part of a large network sunk in a dark cage of trafficking and smuggling not even when one is supposedly feeling free all the way to the golden gate paradise called 'Europe.'

The young lady had a madam who'll be paying for the entire travel as well as the Baba Juju priest so that she'll be covered as she makes this journey to the unknown to a specific ultimate country in Europe she might likely find herself serving a course of paying back all that was spent on her and much more using her body. I mean, literary, she would spend the rest of her uncertain days in Europe to ensure she pays back to her Madam, her chief trafficker, who's also based in Europe. It's not new. It's been like that for decades unchecked until recently when suddenly, the migration crisis was in front and centre of the national political discourse and review, and then, politicians and local traditional custodians at home and abroad are trying to figure out where their fault or role lies in trying to stop this menace that have ripped many young men and women especially the women of their innocence as they must face the world as adults out there in the open wild west.

Having reached home, Osas informed his mother, saying "I have undergone the rituals of fortification." I just got back from Baba's place, said he to his mother. "Okay, how did it go?" Asked his mother. It all went well, said Osas. Good, replied his mother to him. So, now when are you leaving for Kano state. You'll be taking the night Bus, don't forget to book on time. It's cheaper when you book early," said the mother to him. Don't worry mum. The cost of transport is no problem, replied Osas to his mother. "Really?", you are rich. You think, 200,000 naira is enough? It's after you've been through the journey and confronting all its financial demands. Also, arriving in Libya and waiting long for the right time to cross the sea, including feeding and other unforeseen expenses, that's when you know that the money you have on you isn't really enough.

I know all that. Remember, I have been there, done all that. I lived in Italy for seven years before I returned back to Benin City, you mean deported, said his son, Osas to him. Spend your money wisely. If there are jobs there in Libya, don't hesitate to do them. So, you could earn more money to enable you to pay your smugglers who will get you across the waters to Italy, advised the mother. Italy? I want to go to Germany, replied Osas. I know but first you'll land in Italy or Malta but most definitely in Italy. Then they dismissed. During the three days of preparation, he established contacts with that girl he saw by the Juju priest's place as they agreed on the right day and time and the exact bus terminal, where they will be making their trip from.

The day soon arrived, the D-day, when he will begin his journey to the unknown world, A dangerous journey that doesn't guarantee even life. On this morning, all packed up with his suit case. His mother and folks already to bade him goodbye on his journey. He then, called his mother inside her room and gave her 500, 000 Naira (roughly 1,500 dollars). Ohhh, where did you get all this money? What did you do? Asked the mother. Stop, mummy. Just take this money and use it to feed while I'm gone. Where I got it from is not important as he placed the money on the bed in her bedroom, and then opened the door and came out to meet his young ones. His mum came out after him and quickly locked up the door. Of course, she hasn't seen such bulk of money for a long time. First in her heart she was grateful. Secondly, the questions persisted in her mind. Where did my son get this money from? But unfortunately, she didn't have time to chastise his son, as he was already on the road leaving for the Bus station. He put his hand into his pocket and gave his two siblings 5000 Naira each, equivalent of about 15 dollars each. The mother was surprised as do his junior brother and sister. They were all glad and waved him goodbye as he boarded a taxi nearby to bring him to the Bus station. Immediately, he left the mother told the kids give me that money to preserve it for you guys. The young children groaned. No, this is our money, they replied their mother as they went inside the house.

Reaching the park, he met the young lady which they had already planned to make the journey together with, as both of them embraced themselves and waited outside the Bus. Soon, they were called upon to board the Bus as they loaded their luggage into the bus cabin and showed their tickets and then boarded the Night Bus. They both secured a seat together. A comfortable seat in the upper side of the double decker bus. They were glad as they will now take this journey into the unknown. A journey that would ultimately lead them to Europe, if they survive the ordeal. But not yet, at least on this night as they would have to travel first to Kano. The jumping off point to the border country called Niger Republic. They both conversed and got to know themselves better until soon the driver told them they were leaving. It was an all-night journey as they will be in the bus all night possibly arriving at Kano the next morning. It's a journey people were used to. But if one is not comfortable, one is free to take an airplane or flight to Kano. It's sure, he could do that. But for purposes of him getting to meet and knowing her and them making the journey together as promised, he has to go by road, the road journey which are sometimes dangerous as one's journey could end on the road within the country before it even begins. They later slept and when they woke up, they realized they were already in the dusty part of that country. A territory of this country that was close to the Sahel region. Soon, they arrived the station as they disembarked from the bus, picked their bags and proceeded on their journey without wasting time. The journey was long, but it was just the beginning as they must get another vehicle that would transport them to the border where they would cross to begin the second leg of the journey and most important as it leads them into the unknown. They boarded a vehicle which drove them for a couple of hours as they arrived near the border. They came out and made inquiries on how to proceed. They didn't waste time as they boarded another vehicle that would take them across the Nigerian immigration border into the Sahara, but they didn't know it would be a stressful journey that would require energy, time and money even more vehicles than expected as they travel through the Dusty and uncertain Sahara. After a long exhausting trip that took a couple of days, they arrived in Agadez, the jump off notorious city hub of migration, smugglers and people trafficking. They met a smuggler who'll help to negotiate their way through with a pick-up salon vehicle along with several others sitting precariously at the open back. This was after they've met different smugglers who were surrounding and giving them confusing and polarizing information on how to get to Libya and beyond, promising to deliver them across the sea for a certain fee.

In Agadez, they met hundreds of other migrants who were making the exact kind of trip they were making and in the same situation as they were in even as they journey across the Sahara Desert and mountains. It's the most important and dangerous aspect of the journey as you could land or get stranded in a place with the wrong people who might exploit one's weakness and ignorance of that region as many could be duped of their money, while others are misled and forcibly raped. People have fallen prey to these dubious touts, traffickers and smugglers, as they are falsely or forcibly led to the wrong people at the wrong places or wrong location in a strange wide world. But this two have heard all these stories told by many as they were trying not to make the same mistakes or try to avoid as much as possible some of the pitfalls many unsuspecting persons had to fall into, to get violated or ripped off. Out there is a crazy world. Not a world for an innocent girl or boy traveling seeking greener pastures across the Mediterranean but this is what they must face to get the place of fulfillment of hopes. But they were together to make sure they didn't separate, or nothing made them fall out of one another through deception or ill luck. Don't forget they prayed not just daily but regularly as they treaded these paths across the Sahara carefully. It was a Journey that lasted them over three days across this wasteland costing about 500–700 Euros as the boy prayed not to be duped of his money as he banks on this money to get him cross the sea. If not, he may end up involuntarily laboring for many months to earn the required money that will be paid to the smugglers to get him through the high seas or he might fall in the hands of armed militia men who might exploit him.

But he didn't need to do that because he had enough money on him to cover his expenses and possibly the girl too, if he so wishes to. In the pick-up van, they covered their heads and faces to avoid being blinded by the dust. It's rumoured, if your vehicle broke down here in the middle of nowhere, one risk being stranded. Some migrants were reported to be killed by ghosts and dehydration, as some drink their urine to stay hydrated and mobile. After a long torturous journey route and interminable stop at Misrata and Sabha where they paid another 200 Euros in each leg of the journey to board a Chinese made vehicle, they finally arrived at the smuggling hub of Sabratha in Libya after twelve days of an exhausting journey on the road. In Sabha city, it was particularly excruciating for him to learn that many of his country men and women suffered from occasions of slavery in this city, as the men were abducted and forced into labour to pay for their fares across the sea while the women who risk being misled by unsuspecting smugglers and traffickers, were taken to secured hidden locations as brothels, where they were used as prostitutes to service their Arab local militants and others, who rapes them repeatedly, and after months or years of being abducted they're released with a promise, the money they've earned will pay for the smuggling service run by the same militias. This city Sabratha is the most common point of departure for mostly sub-Saharan West African refugees trying to cross the Mediterranean by boat. But in this country, not knowing where to go or how long they might have to tarry in this place, they would later learn that it takes much more than what they had on them as every step of the journey from then or effectively from Niger republic, they were in the hands of smugglers whom they will have to trust to deliver on their promise to get them across to the next destination. In Libya, it was not different as due to the fall of Gaddafi, the crisis had gotten intense as they may have to deal with various rival militant groups of smugglers who have taken over the trade that might be responsible to guide their journey through the last leg of it across to the other side of the world. But that may be a long time away as they have to wait several days to register on the line of those who will cross.

They had to find a smuggler with the knowledge of how to get across. First, they need a place to lay their heads for the night. They stumbled over a local Benin woman, who was glad to know they were natives of her town and decided to take them to where she stays. But the problem is, where she stays was where many other girls and guys stayed as they did all kinds of jobs to survive in this country as well as have sufficient money to travel across when it's time to get into the fishing or inflatable boats to make the dangerous journey. One thing is sure, it's an uncertain fate all the way and they must endure it if they hope to make their dreams come true.

What was wrong with this place was that it's an area where many trafficked and stuck up girls and guys do what ever they can to survive including prostitution. For the guys, who have come a long way from all over west Africa and beyond to camp in Libya waiting for the right time to cross the Mediterranean sea, being here as foreigners, more than ever without a legal stay in that country, they would have to do several illegal things as well as involve themselves willingly or involuntary as teenagers into hard labour which some of them are happy to secure in order to survive during their time in that country. On the other hand, the unlucky travelers are usually picked up by criminal gangs who put them up for auction or sale to higher bidders for forced labour or organ harvesting. However, others may have to get into criminal organizations or run risky criminal errands in order to earn a living. The aspect of the crime or illegal activities these migrants involve themselves in, is the most worrying situation as a lot of them end of cutting short their dreams of traveling further to Europe as some allegedly suspected or caught in crime are jailed in the country's prisons. Even after serving time in jail, many come out and continue the same crime for which they were arrested and locked up in prison because there isn't just any other thing to do. It's either they do what they are doing or beg on the streets.

Today, the situation is much worse as those caught straying by militants are rounded up and arrested, then taken to prison cells set up collectively between Italy and the Libyan militants to ensure migrants are prevented from reaching Europe. Holding cells with inhumane conditions. Mary, the woman who helped them to find a place to lay their heads told them, "In those days during the regime of President Gaddafi, this country was self sufficient. The life here was good. People were paid if they didn't secure jobs and their country's institutions and facilities were working well. But since after he was toppled by France and the United Kingdom backed up by the Americans, the country has fallen or dissolved into a retarded and divided state where criminal militant organizations run various parts of the country as well control parts of their oil wealth. Insecurity is all pervasive as well as crime and economic hardship. Our people used to earn so much money in this country that when they arrive here, they forget their main end destination which Europe or they were just abandoned it because they earned a lucrative lifestyle in various things they were involved in or doing. In fact, they were jobs for many foreigners coming in. It was good here at that time. But it's no longer the case now," She said. "How long have you been here?" Asked Osas. I have been here for three years. I stayed that long because business was good, she said. "You did business here?" What kind of business was that?" Asked Osas further. You should know what I'm talking about, my brother.

"Ojolojolo business," "Akuna akuna," she added. His traveling partner, the girl whispered in his ears explaining what it meant. "Okay, I get it" replied Osas. It pays well. Very well. Some of our girls use this trade to build houses or setup businesses even train their brothers and sisters back home in schools as well as feed our families. It was lucrative. Now, the generosity that have characterized the business for a long time is now eroded just as the stability and moral fabric of the society deteriorates. The breakdown of law and civility. There's abuse now. No regard or respect for the girls. Some are whipped or beaten up. Others are raped. Some denied the rewards for their services. Some girls forced to have sex with dogs, horses, camels and son on. It's just not what it used to be. So, I, just like you guys, want to quit this God forsaken place to a more civilized place in Europe. We believe our business will be better over there, she added.

Of course, the whole talk was about prostitution as some work as harlots in brothels, others on standby in case they were called to offer those services while some line the road sides at night. Some of this prostitution rings are operated by fellow African criminal gangs in association with the Arab militias and pimps. Does your parents. I mean, the parents of everyone here in Nigeria know exactly what their children are doing or where they are? Asked Osas. Yes. We all call our parents and family regularly. Apart from those abducted or put in holding cells, and not allowed to make outside calls, all others basically call their family to inform them of what's going on here. They're all aware. If any family back in Nigeria says, they are not aware, whether they were told or not, then it's a lie. Because generally some of these girls are adequately coached while in Benin of what exactly, they were going to do over in Europe, or the possible risks of rape on the way and the life that might await them in Libya, in case they were not lucky to travel quickly across to Europe," Said Mary. Is she your girl friend? Asked Mary to Osas. You know, you have to endure seeing your girlfriend ultimately doing this job, even as you two are together? Added Mary. "Really?" Replied Osas. But No, she's not my girlfriend. But we are close friends. Then, it's good for you, said Mary, as everyone in the room laughed. Relax, eat and sleep and tomorrow, you may continue your hustle. I will introduce you to a guy, who'll take you to a smuggler, whom you'll make arrangement with concerning your travel across the sea to Europe, Okay? Okay, thank you, replied Osas.

They were offered food and took their bath and then slept. The next day morning, he woke up. Osas demanded as promised that Mary guide them to the Smuggler who'll ultimately ensure their journey to the frontiers of Europe becomes a reality. No, it's too early. Eat something first, said Mary to him. Of course, unlike her companion, Nene, who didn't have sufficient money and had made up her mind to do what everyone was doing in order to survive, He, on the other hand had all the money he needed even in foreign currency. But he must not disclose it to anyone. However, the way he acted could tell anyone there that he was otherwise loaded with cash or had enough to take him through, and that situation might also endanger him, if the wrong people found that out. Although, Nene, his traveling companion didn't have enough, as one trafficked, her Madam located in Rome, Italy had made sure she kept contacts with her and all the people who might influence her course as she travels across to Europe. She gives instructions to her and others in Libya on what to be done, as she ultimately finds her way to Europe. Even if it's never determined how long such trafficked people would wait as the time varies depending on the state of the seas, the readiness of the boat and the agreement entered with the smugglers. When one is generous to the smuggler such a person is given preferential treatment, though not guaranteed as in every other situation pertaining to business life. Soon after the morning engagements, she took them to where they wanted to be. She delivered Osas in the hand of a friend, who'll take him to a well-known smuggler named Ahmed. While, the girl having a name and a number written in a piece of paper showed to her, as they established contact with a smuggling crew in Libya that would facilitate the last leg of her journey, even as made possible by her so called Madam in Italy. After locating and successfully been introduced to Ahmed, they quickly negotiated on what was required of him in order to get across. But because he appeared like every other people coming across who didn't have enough on them, Ahmed didn't border to discuss the path to quick travel even a good boat. Even though, the idea of a good boat doesn't exist as the smugglers care more about their money than the lives at stake. When the time comes, the armed smuggler forces a migrant to travel into a boat whether it's in good shape or not.

He paid in dollars but was careful not to show he had too much on him. But the little he brought out raised the eyebrow of the guy that took him there as he said to him, My bro....you're rich oooo. If you have much more on you, then I don't mind being given some of that. He spoke in pidgin English as they both laughed. When would I leave here to Europe? I mean, when would the boat be ready for me to travel? Osas added. Keep calm. You see, there are many on the list just like you who wants to travel to Europe. You must wait for your turn to travel, He said to him. "And when would that be?" Asked Osas. I don't know. It depends from two weeks to six months or even longer. It's all about the seas and the boat, coast guards as well as the weather not to mention the law enforcement. "You don't want to hurry and go and die?" "Do you?" No, replied Osas. You're lucky you arrived during summer but then, they are a lot of people who came during winter who had to wait for months because the weather was just not good for them to cross the seas. And these people go first. Don't worry you will get across it's just a matter of time and of course control at the sea. He smiled. Okay, replied Osas. How I wish his friend had given him a clue. Maybe he could have avoided the sad situation that might befall him later, if he had to stay longer by paying him more in order to secure another arrangement of traveling earlier.

Remember there is instability in this country as the leader of this country was just recently deposed from power and killed like a common criminal on the streets of his country, which he ruled for 42 years. So, it's a bad time to be in this country as foreigners are hunted and killed especially those who in one way or the other are involved with criminal, separatists or militant organizations or are snitching, those people especially foreigners were quickly eliminated by the militants who governed the streets of several cities of this once beautiful and peaceful country. They then departed there as Osas would have to wait until it was his time to be called to join a boat. As they left, he asked his new friend, "How long have you been in this country? Three years replied his new friend. Where do you work? How do you earn a living here? Here and there. Doing this and that. But one has to do something, if not one will not feed or have a place to lay his head.

Can you show me where I could rent a small room apartment? Where I could sleep and wait until it's time to travel, Said Osas to him. Yes, I already thought of that. I will take you to a friend who knows a landlord where most of our people from Nigeria and Cameroon stays. He'll tell you how much to pay him and then, you could get a place by the end of today, if you settle with him. These are temporary joints, for migrants who are not expected to tarry for a long time in this country. So, you are charged monthly until you get out. He was taken to this block of flats and made to meet with the landlord of the building, who told him the cost of renting a room. He paid immediately and by the end of the day, he had secured a place of his own. To his new friend, this is unusual as people coming try to save every penny they got in order to ensure they don't go hungry. So, such new people with insufficient funds bunk with friends or natives of their country who are nice while they contribute only for feeding. But he was prepared for his journey and now he had to go to where he spent his first night to get his bags to his new place.

Reaching there he told them how everything went and that he got an apartment of his own. I am leaving to my new place, he told them. Nene, if you want to come along, you are free to come and join me. We could stay together. It's big enough for the both of us, said Osas to her. "Is it a big room," that she would eat or a place she could stay to make money, answered one of the girls in the room. Of course, while away, the girl, his travel companion from Nigeria was brainwashed or maybe she expected it and was lucky to have those who will introduce her to the business to start it while there in Libya before going over to Europe to possibly continue with it. It could've been worse, if she was captured or misled by anyone of the Libyan out-lawed pimps, who could take her to join other enslaved girls held captive in enclosures while being repeatedly raped by numerous men. "I don't think I want to join you in your new place. But I will visit you when I have time," Replied Nene. "Really?" replied Osas. He called her to one corner of the room to talk to her privately. Do you want to join these people to do what they are doing? This filthy business? Said Osas to her. Being momentary quiet, I have to stay here. They have decided to allow me stay here. I'm happy about that. I don't want to waste a long time being here for nothing. Or do you have money to give to me? Replied Nene. We could manage with what I have. I brought some money along. We could manage it together until the time we travel across" Added Osas. I don't want to manage here just like that without financial support. If there's something I could do to earn a living here in Libya, I want to explore it and possibly engage it to have enough money. My family need money just as I do. "Do you even know when we are going to leave Libya?" You have a different smuggler taking care of your own stuff, and I have different people arranging mine. So, there's a good chance that we might leave here at different times. So, our paths are crossed but our life and schedule of journey might change everything or may not. Either way, I have decided to stay here with these girls, learn to do what they're doing. Some say, their work pays better. But I promise, we'll meet. I will come over to see you when I have time, Okay? Tomorrow come and pick me to know your place, so that I can always come to see you, if I have to," Said Nene to him. Okay? I will, replied Osas to her as he carried his bag outside, Mary and Nene walked with him out.

He reached home later that day and after putting his stuffs inside the room, he came down the hostel like-building to meet other folks from his hometown to make friends with them as they will be the ones to guide him and possibly show him what he must know while tarrying in this town. He made friends with them and for the next couple of days they were taking him everywhere to know what they do, where to go and to get used to the city. He lets his friends into his apartment as they invite him to theirs to stay and sometimes eat together. One day, the guy who earlier on took him to the smuggler, came to visit his friends who lived there and during their small talk, he remarked, "It looks like this guy is loaded with cash … oooh. The way I see him, he came with lots of money. Another friend retorted in the affirmative …" I think you're saying the truth. This guy brought so much money even in foreign currency. We have taken him to the place he exchanged foreign currency several times for the local one. I think, he still has much more. Maybe, we should pay him a visit when he's not there and take our own share of the dollars he has on him. They joked around. In the coming days, though not organized among them, but two of them would want to execute a job based on that joke to actually steal from Osas. The two guys who planned and, on this day, when he was out, they broke through his door to search his bags as they stole every penny he had on him. All the money gone. They said he doesn't want to work. Now he would find a job, any job and do, and feel what we are feeling." The two thieves muttered within themselves after breaking into his apartment. Of course, they didn't tear the door down to get inside. They once visited him in the house as one of them was discussing with him. The other one took his door key and told them, 'I am coming back soon. Having already planned it. It was a trick. The other guy engaged him with funny stories without Osas suspecting anything was wrong. It took him thirty minutes after which he came back with the key being cut and duplicated by a locksmith. He sneaked the key in placing it on his bed. They waited a couple of days after then. Of course, they were not the only ones visiting him, but he was always careful not to leave anybody in his room for a long time when he was not there. Secondly, he locked his bags with a padlock, so, one can't easily open his bags without him finding out in that limited time he leaves anyone in his house.

Of course, he came back on this day and realized that his bags were forcibly opened with a sharp object possibly a knife or blade.

He noticed it quickly and after going through his stuffs to confirm if he had been robbed, he finally confirmed in the affirmative that truly someone has come into his apartment to steal all his money. He had over 2000 dollars on him and other Nigerian currency he could exchange to get the Libyan currency for his daily use. How come? But the room was locked? Could they have duplicated my room key? He was so confused. He ran down to call someone or explain to the others what had happened to him. Soon, everyone was led into the story of what happened as the tens of West Africans there were asking who could have done that to this guy. Some said, maybe he should investigate all the people he lets into his room. One of them, may have taken that money from his room. A few of the guys that were together when they discussed about him and their suspicion of the fact that he must be rich, started insinuating that it must be one among them who was present there in that room on that day. Some who had pity on him as they realized that he's in for hard times, started secretly questioning all those present in their discussion on that day. But no one agreed to having a clue to what had happened or who broke into his room. When they inquired to know how much he told them approximately 2,500 dollars. They exclaimed. It's terrible. That much money, all gone. So, this guy truly had so much money on him, they rattled among them in a low tone.

Again, the exact money he had lost spread like wildfire throughout that block of flats and everyone kept talking their version of the boy, who he was or must have been to carry so much money on him. "Why didn't you give it to someone to keep it for you or put it in the bank?" Some asked him. As some sympathizers promised to investigate to find out who did that to him. But that line of action might take a long time. However, that happened. Days turned into weeks as they investigated but no one agreed he or she had anything to do with that. It was unfortunate as he was taken care of by friends for the first weeks who gave him food. As they suggested that he should find something to do to earn money. But the fact was that there was nothing honest or legal during these times to do to earn money as the economy was in tatters. They were farms he could be employed in to work but at that time, they didn't have vacancy, so he couldn't be employed. Moreover, there was insecurity everywhere. One of his friends told him, 'look I work for this militia group as handy boy and informant. My work is dangerous. You could be killed. But it pays good.' Think about it. If you're comfortable with that then, I will take you to my head and introduce you to him, said his friend to him. "What other thing can one do there?" He asked. The other thing to do, which I don't advise is for you to handle a gun and be ready to kill as a separatist militant. You're not a citizen and you don't speak the language which makes you an easier target to sell out or dispose off. "These people don't like us Nigerians and black west Africans," he said to him. "But are they Nigerians doing that kind of Job?" Asked Osas. Yes, a few around the country. There are many people from all over West Africa who have been here for a long time. They speak the language and are into all kinds of things in this country.

Then I'll like to handle the gun. Just take me to him when you have time. I want to work for the militia organization. I know if I'm loyal it will pay more," said Osas. Really? "Did you mean to say what you just said?" Can you handle a gun or shoot? Asked his friend Opepe. I need to do something. If not, I might be thrown out of my condo soon. And where do I go, if that happens? "Must I squeeze myself into your room with you guys, when you're already feeding me?" No, I don't want to live this life anymore. Instead of begging or stealing, I should go do something even though they're outlawed group and are hunted by the military and law enforcement groups of this country. I believe, if they survived, I will survive too. So, please, take me to him. And yes, I have handled a gun before. You know how life is, back home. I have done this and that to survive before, replied Osas. Okay, relax, calm down, I will call him. He will give us time to meet him. He's always busy. It's in the next city. Basically, outskirts of Sabratha. It's tasking, I must add. They will need you all the time. You may not live here anymore. I come here often, because I am a snitching mouse and the errands guy. So, I could go anywhere undetected. Moreover, before I forget and before you plunge into this devil's deal or sit on his tale, you should know that you can't trust anyone of them. Because, one of them might reveal your identity to the Police or the government. Once that is done, your situation is in jeopardy. Even, your ambition of traveling abroad might come to an end because if you were ever caught you could go to jail for a long time or be killed. But on the other hand, you have already paid to travel across, so, the day you're called upon, disappear, don't tell anyone and come over here, get your things and enter the boat and get away, right? But make sure your boat is not captured and you arrested and taken back. Because when you do, and they discovered you didn't tell them the truth, they could harm you.

Moreover, if you tell them, you are traveling out to Europe, they might not employ you to work with them knowing you might not stay with them for a long time. They are looking for people they could trust who could be loyal and serve them not for one or two months but for much longer. If you do, you'll be rewarded. Do you still want to be part of this group after hearing all this, said his friend to him? "If there's anything, I'm even hardened to do this." Just like you said, when the time comes, and I'm called. I would secretly get away to come and join the boat with others abroad. Okay, your mind appears made up already. But don't ever tell me, I didn't warn you. He made the call, luckily got his chief and explained the situation to him about a guy who came a month ago but wants to join them. He told him that the guy has worked as a militant before and could handle a gun. Lastly, he was going to stay longer. Not traveling soon. After explaining it to his commander, he was immediately invited by their chief who wanted to meet him the next day. After dropping the phone, he told him you're lucky. He had asked us to come. You might get in. But watch your back. It's dangerous. If you're not betrayed by them, you could get killed by the soldiers or law enforcement in any occasion of an encounter during your criminal operations. Their group had tried to make peace with the government several times, but it failed. So, they are hunted and wanted by the soldiers, so, if you are not careful, you could get killed without fulfilling the purpose to which you left Benin city. They along with other militant groups since the fall of Gaddafi had threatened the peace and security of this country as well as divided this country into their territorial holdings.

The next day evening according to set schedule time of meeting his boss, Osas friend Opepe brought him over to his militant boss in the nearby city. Reaching there, they waited. Soon they were led in as the both of them had audience with the chief of this terrorist organization. "I know about Boko-Haram. Are you one of them?" The militant commander asked. No, answered Osas. But I have been part of the Niger Delta freedom fighters. A group known as MEND or Movement for the Emancipation of Niger Delta. A group amongst many others that fought to emancipate the oil region of Nigeria from the domination and suppression by the Nigerian government, He added. Okay, I know them. That's what we do too. We are freedom fighters. Many of our guns and men go to Nigeria to fight for Boko-Haram. I am for freedom. But I'm against their ideals of denying education to the common people. Our organization don't have problem with the common people unless they betray us to the government or soldiers. Like us, Boko-Haram do the opposite. They kill and enslave the common people. That's wrong. However, since they need our help and guns with the money they send to us, we are obliged to support their cause by sending guns across to them." All good. Now, you said, you want to be part of us. Your friend from Benin city told me you are all geared up to be part of us. "Are you sure, you are ready for this job?" It's demanding. It needs training and you need to understand the language. Perhaps, you have the training but not the language which is very important to us because most of our people communicate with Arabic. Your friend here has been with us for a while now and he could speak our language because he has lived here now for five years, said the Commander. "I can learn, Sir", responded Osas.

I don't doubt that for a second. "How long do you intend to stay in Libya?" Asked the militant chief. For as long as possible. As long as you let me work for you guys," replied Osas. I know you all came here in order to cross the sea to Europe, but some end up staying much longer than expected. So, that might happen to you still if you want. But wanting to be part of us is a long-term thing. You need to resolve your mind within to that fact. Other than that, we don't want you, said Commander Hassan. I am ready to commit to this group, if you give me a chance, Sir," Replied Osas. Okay, good, replied Hassan. "Can you call me tomorrow, Opepe?" Said Commander Hassan. If you can start next week. Then we'll make a place for you and let others know about your coming, he added. Okay, thank you, Sir. I'm grateful, responded Osas to him. He then left along with Opepe. Reaching home, his friend told him, Osas, it was a successful trip. I will now leave and go to work. Next week on the exact date and time, as he has told you, you need to be there. But like I said, it's a dangerous game. Be careful and any day, you're called to enter your boat and go to Europe. Just quietly escape and join the boat. That's the only guarantee you have to living longer, Okay?" Spoke his friend to him. Thanks brother. I will do as you say, responded Osas. In the coming week, and at the exact date, he went alone, and on reaching there, he was welcomed in. As their Commander Hassan designated a junior lieutenant to show him to his room. The same person will train him on offense and defense art of war combat tactics, military strategies including handling of bigger guns as well as other techniques of strategic defense against an enemy gunfire. He was told by the junior lieutenant that "our primary objective is to direct every militia operation towards a clearly defined, decisive and attainable goal. Go into an offensive to seize, retain and exploit the initiative, which in this case are the oil fields in order to stay afloat while concentrating combat power at the decisive place at any given time." Most importantly, our clear enemy is the government and the military or security forces, and we have to always put them at a disadvantageous position through a flexible application of our principles using the carrot and stick method.

In the next couple of weeks, he must undergo this daily training as he has now left his life wholly to the hands of this group who sometimes engage in kidnapping but rarely. They alongside other groups control in part the oil wealth of Libya as they illegally exploit, drill the oil and sell to international organizations at a reduced rate. With such money coming into their coffers, they sustain their terrorist entity. He landed in late July 2013 at a very good time to sail across the seas. But if he couldn't make it during that period of summer extending the fall, it will get even more difficult to take that trip unless those who take the risks are very sure, they are the European frontex organization, aid groups and other naval presence out in the seas who might spot them early, in case of distress, come over to rescue them. He stayed with them for two months as during that period he learned a little Arabic language, and was astute, committed to their cause and to his security as well. Let say, he was loyal and liked by a few of his junior commanders, who liked having him around him. He tells jokes and was funny using broken English which they understood. Also, very committed as they saw it with their eyes. But he was also very intelligent and coning as during that three months, he was in touch with his friend outside who regularly kept in touch with the smuggler pressing him against better reward if he facilitates and expedites the process at a faster pace so that his friend could get away.

Opepe was worried for his friend and brother being sucked into that mindless killing group, and for what? Just to survive? On the other hand, his friend Osas was making money. Let's say he had enough at this time to quit the group. But though that idea comes to mind, he dares not take it to task or implement it as he might be endangering his life, if he left and was still found loitering around the cities of Libya. Especially the port city of Sabratha where he could easily be found out, captured, tortured even killed. If that scenario occurs then he may only endanger his life as his only option is to await his call and hope, that call comes in sooner before they will go for the next operation against sabotage of the oil government facilities. A situation that when encountered with the country's army could leave several dead. Remember no life is important to these people. As one dies another is either coerced into their group or led in willingly for the sake of the reward.

Luckily, in the beginning of the third month of his stay, a call came in but that was an inauspicious time to travel as the weather at this time and date was harsh and unpredictable as the flimsy fishing boats and ships they use don't have navigational equipment to keep in touch with the sea watchers and coast guards on the other end to guard against wild climatic or weather situations that might arise while on the seas and put them in jeopardy. A call came in at one night and he was told it was a convenient time to travel. When he asked, when the next boat might come in, he was told in a week, depending on the weather and sea security situation at that time. Because like his smuggler, they were several other smugglers plying the same route. It's a lucrative business and everyone wants a pie out of its goodies. The thousands of deaths of desperate migrants are not the least their concern. To them, you need a service, it was provided. Whatever happens to you on the seas, is not their business. They are not culpable to such disaster as the victims knew exactly what they were getting themselves into. On the eve of this day he was called on at about 10 p.m., in the night, and told to prepare that they were going to leave with a prepared boat on the next morning. He didn't hesitate. He waited until it was late at night. When the last buses were leaving to the port city. He then left their condo just with his money and essentials on his pocket. He journeyed through the desert outskirts where this garrison-like training base was located. He reached the park in less than two hours and immediately boarded a bus. It drove a couple of hours and soon he was at his destination in Sabratha. Knowing fully well they were to depart for Europe that morning. He went to knock at his friends' room in his former residence. He was led in, welcomed as he told them I am leaving later this morning. Although, he tried to sleep he couldn't. In the early hours, they all moved as group along with those he knew living in the same block of flats, who were part of this trip. That morning they reached there and saw this inflatable boat not so good looking. They didn't have time to complain as one of them already drilled on how to pilot forward was told to make sure he takes over when the pilot later gets out. This boat was to take them to the point in the sea where a bigger fishing boat was waiting. During this period unlike now they were not much Libyan coast guards that watches over the seas paid for by the European union nations who are troubled and divided over the number of influx of people are coming into their countries.

They started their journey in this boat alongside others with over four hundred people packed themselves in a not so good nor large inflatable boat. After a short time, they reached the high seas. They boarded a larger Boat. Among them were pregnant women, babies, minors, the wounded, escapees shot and other tortured people by the Libyan smuggling gangs. They must endure the many hours on the Mediterranean Sea as their journey had kicked off even as some were already actively engaged in prayers. After reaching a certain point outside the shores of Libya, the captain fled the ship and assured them of their safety that they should keep calm. "On the other side, you'll be picked up by the European coast guards, aid agencies or commercial vessels," he remarked. On the seas and during a stormy period that a lot of people feared to travel. Not just because it's an unsuitable period to travel across the sea but also when the smugglers ignore the warnings of the meteorological data services concerning the time suitable to move on the seas due to their insatiable quest to make money from the heads of strangers whose lives mean nothing to them, then it makes them cruel.

However, traveling through the sea at anytime is dangerous. At every level of the boat journey they were scares and frights, as they prayed for their boat not to stop on the way for any reason whatsoever or for seas not to surge as that was their biggest fear. The surging waves of the sea could endanger their lives or sink the ship since they were over-packed. Soon, in the midst of fear and prayer for safety, a friend began telling horror stories of a boat that sunk in the high seas. This fishing Boat was carrying migrants but being over packed in an unlikely weather and under a precarious circumstance, the passengers perished. Life jackets they had on meant nothing when help doesn't arrive on time and when needed, the story teller said. The story continued. We heard there this particular boat, passengers of the boat reaching the middle of the sea the boat seized to function. The fuel had dried up. As the boat with all its passengers got weary and was beginning to sip in water and couldn't move but drifted from one corner of the sea to another being beaten by the waves. It got to a point that there was disagreement between several groups of the passengers as many of them couldn't swim but they decided to let some people out of the boat for the boat to stabilize, if not they all would eventually perish.

After a long argument, some voluntarily jumped into the seas but those were those who could swim holding onto a few protective vests. The problem with this was that, you could swim to an end when you know where exactly you're going to and the distance of the journey not far outstretched. But this boat was at least twenty-four hours near any border. So, those who decided to go into the water although not completely aware of their fate were doomed to perish. But they jumped anyway. Immediately they jumped, a few of the guys on board became fierce and aggressive as they began forcing people to enter into the water or be thrown into it.

In the midst of the squabble of a hungry, confused and dazed out people in a boat that was not functioning and was hardly near any shore, they forcibly carried passengers and threw them overboard. Even mothers and babies were not spared in the onslaught. It was brutal, but they had to do it or, so they said if not they were all doomed. At this time, the situation was rowdy and pitiful as several weak and crying passengers were forced to jump or be thrown in, as those who refused were bundled up and flung into the seas. In the end, half of all those in the boat were forced to go into the seas. By the way, many of those perished not long after as they could only hang on for so long. Though almost half were left, the situation of the boat was deteriorating on minute basis, as more people were crying.

Everyone was crying apart from those perpetrating these worst crimes. At a point they didn't care who was flung into the sea or not as many of all the people either jumped willingly or were forcibly flung into the sea without protective vests. In the end, only a few were left including these guys who were committing this act, thinking by doing that the pressure on the boat to allow for stability and floating of the boat would be lifted or released.

But at this point it was a lost cause as the weather was bad and the surge of the sea grew, slamming the boat from one end to another until finally flipping the boat upside down as everyone at this point was let into the stormy waters. They all perished at this place and point with no help from anywhere. Even, the experienced swimmers at this point couldn't escape the torrent fury of the seas as it deluged the boat along with the passengers in it. It was reported that out of the nearly four hundred and fifty persons that were part of the trip, only one or two who hanged on in inflatable floating rubber other than those who swam for many kilometers, some of which eventually exhausted and gave up, that were consequently sighted and picked up by a vessel after over 24 hours swimming. They then transported the lucky few to the European shores. For Osas, it was scary and a story to dread especially as a passenger in the same kind of journey on the same sea route that have gulped the lives of many of his country men and women who made the same journey months and years before he made his.

After many hours of the boat steering across the seas and stretching up to three days and nights, they were eventually spotted by the European coast guards who made a quick effort to rescue them into a bigger vessel. According to Osas, it was a thing of joy, the very moment we saw hope from a distance as hope also spotted us, as we screamed and eventually we were all one by one rescued onto the bigger ship, a situation that had many of us jumping into the water to get across onto the safer boat. They all were finally brought out of the old fishing boat onto the European commercial vessel, which eventually contacted the European coast guards. They were given coats, blankets and other forms of dressing for protection against the cold as they were also given food even as they were all sailed to the Italian coast of Sicily.

Reaching close to the Sicilian port of Catania had several of them singing the Hallelujah song of praise to God for granting them a safer passage across the same old enemy sea that have swallowed many of their peers, relatives, friends or migrant strangers like them who were fleeing war, persecution and hunger to a place of sanctuary. They all sang with a loud voice, watched by their rescuers, who were wondering why in the world would anyone one risk their lives across the dangerous sea only to seek a better life that's often not guaranteed. A familiar phrase used by many of the rescuers. Why are these people desperate to come to Europe? That was what was ringing in their hearts as they watched the migrants sing their hearts out in joy for finally reaching their place of hope, if there was any place as such on earth. With fanfare they were all welcomed as the ship with over 400 refugees rescued from the Mediterranean to Italy arrived and docked. One pregnant refugee woman has gone into labour and doctors rushed her to the hospital. She is not the only person needing medical attention. One man is stretchered away with two gunshots wound to his leg and arm. Amid the agony and distress, were a stream of families, toddlers, children, happy minors, women and men who were elated. Those attended to and allowed to come out fell to their knees, threw themselves on the ground, kissing the tarmac before getting back up with joy, happy to be in Europe and most of all, on dry land.

The process of disembarking is long and tedious. Medics wearing face masks and infection suits line up to examine the new arrivals, checking temperatures and looking into their mouths. Afterwards is the Police checks and photographing. The asylum seekers pass through the medical checks to a network of tents, to have their bodies and bags searched and to join a queue for fingerprinting and identification. Even phones are checked for names and numbers of smuggling gangs. They are finally led into the port's car park, where waiting buses took them to reception centres to apply for a right to stay in Italy. The entire process is slow and agonizing even as they were being prepared to be registered or processed into a new life in Europe. On board were Pakistanis, Afghans, Syrians, Libyans and other West Africans, including girls trafficked for prostitution as well as others with horrible stories of hardship and violence. Here are they now to a new life that will have them seeking asylum in an entirely new system and culture which they might learn to inculcate including the language, if they hoped to ever integrate into this new society. However, if integration is what a refugee or migrant will pay to achieve the life he or she dreamed of, then it's a little price of sacrifice to pay. But that is a long way ahead. A long way to get there often wrought with challenges that present themselves including mental distress, social dejection, depression, isolation, despair, loneliness, sense of unfulfillment and the immigration processing, sucking the joy out of the beautiful experience of true integration, which is always offered by their hosts with a grain of salt.

CHAPTER TWO

A NEW LIFE IN EUROPE

Having reached Europe. In Italy, there began the process. It's a long process. But first they were given a place to lay their heads for the night. An accommodation was provided where depending on the size of the room up to four to six persons shared a room. Each day there were expected to have three meals a day. A rich meal for the migrants but that was far and hardly what these migrants risked their lives for. Although, it takes time to process anything involving migrants in Europe as if the authorities in Europe think life is indefinite but these migrants along with other distress boats rescued off the coast of Italy were processed. But in the next two weeks they were provided places, an asylum home to stay and adjust to the new environment. Osas was particularly happy as he was given a place to share with his fellow Nigerian folks. In exactly three weeks, after his screening and clearing as an unaccompanied minor, they were given identity cards as refugees and were eventually distributed across the country. He was sent to a youth centre in Turin along with an accompanying official guardian. Thousands of Nigerian migrants like several other west African countries in Italy find it difficult to be granted asylum. Earlier he had heard it rumored even among the officials in Sicily that if they want to go to other countries, they were free to go there after being processed and given official documents.

The same sentiments echoed by several of the Syrians and Afghans he met over there who were all willing to go to other countries including Sweden and Germany. Immediately after being processed and assigned to go to Turin, he along side a Syrian he met there and a couple from Senegal that have been in Italy for several years but now willing to relocate to Germany set out to make this Journey to Germany as the country of their choice. For his female travel companion from Nigeria to Libya, and consequently to Italy, she was also assigned to Turin, a place she went to start off a new life in Italy. Reaching there, she was welcomed by her Madam who was all the way on the phone communicating with her.

She has arranged for a place for her in the city away from the refugee's hostel, in the city where she would stay with other girls she has tutored into prostitution. Her Madam lives in Rome but traveled to Turin to receive her into her trade.

Nene would resign herself to starting her life into a lifestyle which she has somewhat practiced in the past few weeks she tarried in Libya. Unlike many others trafficked persons who in the earlier times, were issued a visa at the Italian embassy and they flew straight from Murtala Mohammed Airport, Lagos to Italy without an idea into what they were going to do in that country but hoped their lives would change for the better as some were promised good jobs such as in the Hair Salon, restaurant or in the fashion industry. But were surprised as they awoke into a strange life where they were forced into a filthy life with their pimp Madam practically tearing off their clothes and giving them to some strange sex hungry clients to sleep with. Nene, on the other hand, was well aware of what she would be doing here in Turin. She has been briefed and let's say she has practiced enough to guide her in her reaction to her new Italian clients. That night didn't pass as her madam who came traveled all the way from Rome to Turin because of her wanted to see her conversant with her new work in order for her to recoup her finance she spent on her travel from Nigeria to Europe.

Although, she earned some money back in Libya, part of that money was sent back to Benin City in Nigeria to be used to take care of her folks. But now it will be a full-time job as she was advised by her Madam, *"if you want to earn enough money to pay me and to save for yourself and your poor family back in Benin city, you need to resolve your mind to working even extra time, for that's the only way to make it here in Italy and survive at the same time."* It's a hard world and you need to get used to it. If it was easy back in Nigeria non of you would have bothered yourselves to come here to lead this life. "Once again, like your friends have been doing, she said to her, some of them for over three to ten years already, some of which have finished their payments and earning a decent life with their own money, you too could be like that if you obey me and pay up, and I mean regularly," she added. And if you ever think of escaping, let's just say, no one would run after you but think of the Juju ritual pact you'd entered into with Baba in Benin City. With that she meant the Witch doctor who tore her skin with evidence of physical marks and a covenant she agreed to and laying fearful curses on her, if she ever fails to fulfill her part of the agreement.

Having spoken to her, that night she was served with three men, who were partly the customers of the other girls but wanted her since she was a fresh meat. I call it meat, because looking at her, that's all they saw, a piece of flesh to be had, toyed with, or rubbished with no sympathy or tinge of humanity for those migrants and their welfare, and so could be said about the authorities too. She slept with three men separately, that night some of which invited her to their homes, picking her up with their vehicles, and finally returning her back in the morning, because she was new. Returning that morning she was asked by her friends, how was it? Did it go well? "Well," She responded. Already she had been coached by one of the girls in the apartment who took a keen interest on her. "One of them wanted to have anal sex with me but I said No. I resisted him," Said Nene to her. "Really?" answered her friend. "So, you mean to tell me, you've never done it?" Yes, "I swear I've never done it." But the man understood. But told me, I need to learn to perform anal sex. He said, I could earn more money if I agreed to it." Added Nene. Well, my advice to you is that don't do what you don't want to do. But also, to succeed in this business you have to indulge in the men's perverted sexual preferences and fantasies including entertaining whips, chains and pain when asked of you by a wealthier client. Then, you get paid good money", Advised her friend.

Of course, she has to pay for her new accommodation, as the madam returned that morning to collect much of the money she made that night, while urging her to be straight with her, and not to try anything smart or stupid. "I am watching you, be good" She said to Nene. After her Madam left and lying on the bed that morning, even as her friends went out for the same business, it dawned on her, that for the rest of her new life in Europe, she might be dedicated to a new job, an abhorred or less than desired way of life even for the standard of the society she now finds herself in or the society she hails from. The same life lived by thousands of Nigerian and West African girls in Italy, and apart from the fact that several have been saved from this filthy world she's plunged into, many other girls have made their peace with it for a long time, and see it like any another job they have to do, to put food the table and that of their family back in Africa.

Osas, on the other hand, and his new friends immediately set out on this Odysseus journey without wasting time and without going to Turin, he alongside others left for Germany. They boarded a train to Germany. After several hours in the train they finally arrived in Southern Germany in Munich as the Police came into the train and interrogated them. They reported that they came from Italy and that they wanted to seek Asylum in Germany. They were eventually guided on what to do and where to go to. The train finally stopped at the Train station called Munich Bahnhof. They alighted and boarded a taxi, that took them to BAMF headquarters. This is the German immigration department and centre for refugees and migrants that processes all newcomers who intends to seek asylum in that country. Once again, they arrived late and were led to accommodation near to the headquarters processing centre to spend the night. The next morning, they got to the office again to continue the process. They were eventually processed as they were finger-printed, photographed and scanned. As for him, the local youth office was contacted, to sort out his accommodation and other proceedings during the asylum procedure. The youth office then immediately initiated a clearing procedure. The first step of this procedure is often the First Screening, as it's called, which includes a medical examination and some tests for age assessment.

A couple of days prior, was his Nineteenth birthday. But he had a choice to tell them his true age or do as he was earlier told by his colleagues back in Italy. He was told, "If he used his true age of 19 years, it might be difficult for him on the long run to be granted Asylum or benefit from other state social services including education." In Germany, Asylum under 18, makes you legally a minor. And just as he did in Italy. He took two years out of his age in order to be processed as an unaccompanied minor. Already the documents he got from Italy showed his age at 17. Usually, one will be transferred to one of the 16 states within two weeks of one's arrival. During the clearing process, the foreigner's office will clarify his residency status. Of course, he looked young. In fact, he looked sixteen, so his examiners didn't have any reason to doubt him. They are other asylum seekers who take out up to seven years from their original age, it's a question of survival, he was told. After all, there was no way of ascertaining it since they didn't have passports on them. If examined and confirmed, it's a life saver because then, the minor will avoid all the stress, his fellow asylum seekers go through to be granted asylum or deported and will eventually be afforded education. Under 18 years, he was restricted from making legal decisions, as he couldn't apply for asylum personally without a guardian.

Afterwards, he was given a temporary identity card preparing him along with his new Syrian friend to another location that might house them on permanent basis after about two weeks in Munich. He was sent to Wuezburg, a city in Bavaria in Southern Germany. He arrived and was given accommodation by the Youth Welfare Office (Jugendamt). A Hostel accommodation for youth refugees. The Youth welfare office and family court are responsible for finding him a guardian. He was assigned an official guardian, an employee of the

Youth Welfare Office to supervise him. To permanently remain in Germany, the guardian applied for a residence permit on behalf of him for humanitarian reasons. He opted to live with a family rather than in the youth centre as he told his official guardian. After a long search, he got 'Foster Parents', as Adoptive Parents were hard to come by, who accommodated him. They didn't have exclusive parental rights to care for him as biological parents do, but they would decide about everyday life issues including health, language, integration and education. His Syrian friend, on the other hand, was an adult so their terms of process though the same would eventually follow different paths. He stayed in this accommodation provided for young migrants and refugees by the Youth Welfare Office until his foster parents who'll oversee him as he starts his preparatory educational and language studies came to pick him up to his new home, their home as his foster care parents. He didn't waste time as he alongside his foster parents registered in a local school and he started attending his preparatory classes.

Osas soon was admitted into a language school in Volkhochschule to begin a course to study and speak German that will eventually prepare him for an Ausbildung training when he is 18 years. It's not easy learning to speak and write German, if you deny it ask the many other thousands of foreigners or immigrants of other nations who have been in Germany for many years some spanning decades. They'll tell you, it's not easy learning to speak German especially in the right accent except you come to Germany as a child. At the age of 19 years, his head was already filled with other things, including the responsibility of providing for his family back at home, so, in that position, unlike 12 years old, it's hard to learn the language quickly. That was the situation he finds himself in, but he must strive to speak and write the language if he has to go further in his pursuit of education. Of course, he communicated with German at home. That might help him to quickly adapt. In the next year, he was able to speak more than a few words, and could communicate with his fellow colleagues at school. He was admitted starting a Berufsschule, a vocational school where in the next three to five years, he would learn more of the language, and choose the kind of course he would study, while being prepared for the professional world with the last three years of his education devoting to the profession in life he choses to. He was committed to his studies, and after the first two years, he chose and began his vocational training that will see him study Nursing.

He met and made friends with new people some of which were foreigners like himself and most of them Germans while into his full-time professional course. He strives not only to study the language or profession but the culture as he went out with new German friends and went to their parties when invited. In his class, there was a girl, named Ann Mueller in school who was particularly fond of him as he was unusually brilliant and shy, as soon after studying closely in school, they began inviting one another to their social circles, a means that saw them mingle more and became friends with each other. They were soon noticed in their class to be inseparable as they did everything together. One day, he went over to the African Shop in Theatrestrasse, Wuezburg to get some African foodstuffs including Plantain, yam, palm oil, Egusi and bitter leaf for a local Nigerian delicacy. He met a couple of new friends as they discussed their challenges on areas concerning the affairs of their intimate love life with locals.

One of the guys asked him bluntly, "do you do oral sex with your girl including licking her vulva?" What do you mean by that? Osas asked. I mean, "her clitoris," as others laughed. The point is to stimulate her biggest sex organ. I have never done it. Is that even healthy? Asked Osas. Yes, I kiss her thighs, and let her feel the sexual anticipation while stimulating her feelings with sweet words," Added Osas. Look here, my brother! Hmmm, as he expressed some mixed facial emotions. That's not enough. 'Make her feel the Koko.' Who cares if it's healthy or not? That's what most of the ladies here want, if not all. If you ask everyone here in this shop, if they did it before coming to Germany. Most will say No, they didn't. Just like some migrants started smoking in Europe, sometimes for flimsy reasons such as to please their partner or in order to fit in, in social circles.

You see, here, it's survival of the fittest. *'If you don't make her happy, her love might go down in the shadows, expire, and with the loss of interest, she might dump you and look for another person to satisfy her.'* They're lots of guys out there to give her that pleasure. How long have you been together? Asked the African guy while seriously engaging Osas in Pidgin English language. "About six months," answered Osas. I bet she's still hanging on because of the size of your manhood. "You know German girls only love African guys because of that and no other thing," he babbled on. It's stereotype. It's common around this country, he added. Why are you saying all these to me? Asked Osas. Because I figured you're new and you need to understand the nitty gritty. Thank you, replied Osas as he left the shop. In the coming days, as he met Ann, his girlfriend, having earlier on, consummated their relationship, he tried to practice what he was told in the shop and surprisingly it worked, as that boosted his sex life. Not to mention, the girl played an important role to get the guy to hit the right spots to achieve perfection on that part.

One day, in 2016, three years into his stay and studies in Germany he went to Kiliani fest, a popular festival event hosted by the city tourism board, where he met a group of friends, some of whom he knew, and in that group, he met a girl whom they communicated and soon, they exchanged numbers. In the next coming days, they would communicate via WhatsApp. He devoted to his studies just as to his now waning friendship with Ann and other social meetings he had with other male friends, some of which were geared at chasing their scholarly dreams and the girls. In the spring of 2017, his last year of studies, after not being in communication with that girl for over a year, the girl wrote him and asked if he was interested to meet her for a drink in a popular restaurant in the city. A very familiar behavior of preference for young people who are looking forward to a rebound after a failed love or romantic relationship. They did and later that evening he invited her to his place. At this point in time, he already hired his own private apartment where he lived. He was still communicating with Ann, but they have for over a year now fallen out of love with one another. She came along, and he entertained her, making her comfortable as they chatted off, laughed and enjoyed one another's company. The next week, they planned to meet again, and as she came over to his place. Having expected her, she knocked and in a captivating moment he opened the door. "Hey," she said to him. "Hey," he responded right back. You're beautiful. She walked in gently, starred at his eyes with weakness, sending the right signals of soft emotions, he leaned closer, grabbed her and they kissed. At that moment they started a new path and relationship, as they made out that night, an act that would see them hooked onto one another even as his communication with Ann stopped. Of course, he learnt a lot from his former relationship with Ann including romantic gestures. Lisa, the new girl had just finished his University degree in the Wuezburg University and was ready to enter into a long-term relationship with her new man that would see her think on the line of being married and pregnant to have a child. Here is Osas, the lucky fellow, who learned after three months of their relationship that the new girl was pregnant. As he woke him up one morning with a kiss and message to her dear one, saying the words, darling. Yes, he replied. I think I am pregnant. "Really," responded Osas. I believe so. But I would go over tomorrow to see the Doctor to confirm it. 'Beautiful, what a wonderful news I just heard this morning from you.' I love you, Baby, he added. I love you too, she responded.

He encouraged her to keep the child and she agreed because she had already made up her mind to keep the child, and they loved each other. Having such understanding, she decided to introduce him to her parents, who didn't really like the guy, maybe it's because of how he looked or the career he chose. But her parents were not unique in not cherishing their children's foreign lovers as statistics has it that more parents of the German young adult girls falling in love with foreign or migrant men especially from Africa don't always approve of it. Not because they don't like foreigners being their children's lovers, on the contrary, they do but let it not be an African migrant, black or Arab, as the case may be. But if history tells the parents anything, most of their children always ended up doing the exact opposite of what their parents asked of them. However, not all, as some due to the pressure put on them by their parents and friends might make them to take another approach or step back to evaluate their relationship with this foreigner, whom he or she loves but his or her parents or friends don't like or approve of.

Her situation was different as she was already pregnant with his child and would want nothing but to be with the father of her unborn child. In the coming days, he proposed marriage to her with a ring. She was ecstatic, because she loved him, and she wanted nothing more than to be his wife. They later planned and hired a bigger apartment which both of them stayed even as they expected to welcome a new child of love in their midst in the coming months. One day, Osas got ignited with the thoughts of Nene, his travel companion with whom they made the journey together to Europe. The young girl who was caught up in the sex trafficking ring in Turin, Italy. He went to the city centre to collect some stuffs and met a couple of newbies or new asylum seekers just posted to Wuezburg. All of a sudden, he was involved in a discussion with one of them concerning an Edo girl from Benin, Nigeria whom they traveled together but she decided to stay over in Italy. "I asked her to accompany me to Germany, but she refused and rather opted to remain in Turin. She told me, her Madam, might hunt her down and harm her, if she defied the covenant contract she entered into with the Juju priest to be loyal to her Madam, while consenting to death, if she ever failed to fulfill her own part of the pact." He told them. "Her situation isn't unique," replied the new guy. But if she wanted to run away she could have done so. They are a lot of girls rescued and rehabilitated from that illicit trade of sex trafficking. They are not dead. The Juju cult didn't kill them. Though, some suffered from psychological and mental problems including body itches, voices in their heads, haunted dreams and nightmares but they still survived. So, she too can, if she wants to. One thing about the sex trade is that when once one is started on it and hooked like a "spirit," it's always hard to stop, even if one wanted to. That's where aid and other non-governmental organizations tasked with helping sex trafficking victims to get reinstated come into play." Said the new experienced asylum seeker from Italy.

Just as they were discussing in the midst of others in the African shop, one of them asked Osas. What is her name again? Nene, is her name. I don't know her second name. I never asked. "Maybe, I know her," said one of the newbies. In Munich, in the Asylum seekers temporary hostel was a girl from Italy. I met her once and we spoke for a couple of hours in the native Edo language. She gave me her number but told me she had been there for three weeks already and that she is relocated being to Schweinfurt, a small city in Bavaria. When did you guys leave Nigeria? What year? He asked Osas. 2013 and we arrived Autumn of that year in Italy. I've not seen her for over four years," Replied Osas to the guy. Exactly. That was the same year she told me she came into Italy. Once again, she might be the one. I'll check her number out and give to you to call and confirm if she's the one, Ok?" He added. I'll really appreciate that. He checked the numbers. A second, please, he said. Yes, I found it. You got your phone on you? Yes, answered Osas. Shoot. 01575544881-Nene. That's the number. Thanks a lot, said Osas to the guys in Pidgin English and then left.

Reaching home his fiancée was out. He tried the number and luckily it worked. It rang the first time. No one answered. He called again the second time. This time there was a response. Nene, answered. "Who's this, please?" My name is Osas Erebuwa. Is this Nene? Asked Osas. Yes. I am Nene. Osas? The same one we traveled together from Nigeria? Asked Nene. Yes, I am. Answered Nene. Wonderful, I thought I might never see you again. How did you get my number? Asked Nene. It's the work of God. An Edo boy who just came from Italy gave me your number. He met you in a refugee's hostel in Munich, he said to me, and you gave him your number. He gave it to me, not knowing if it's you but said I should try. It might be you after I described you to him. So, where are you now? Asked Osas. In Schweinfurt. Just close-by. I live in Würzburg, a stone throw from where you are now, added Osas. Nice, then, maybe, we should plan to meet each other. Can I come to visit you in the coming week? Are you living alone? Asked Nene. No, actually, I have someone I am living with in the house. My wife to be. I am engaged to her. She's carrying my child already. Tell me about you, what happened in Italy? And what are you doing there now? Asked Osas as he was curious. My long-lost brother, she muttered. The same thing I was doing in Italy is the same thing I am doing here now. I just got employed in a brothel. Today, is my day off, said Nene in a distressed tone. I can't believe this. They allowed you to work? Do you have a working permit? Asked Osas. Yes, I got it two months ago. You mean, you got a working permit and all you could think of, is going to work in a brothel as a prostitute? It's just crazy. Sorry, for my reaction. But I thought after all these years doing the same thing and you are now here, perhaps you'd be doing something else to earn a living like every other person. Maybe get an education or something. He spoke to her with a tone of disappointment and anger that could be felt in his words. Don't judge me, my brother. Blame life. You think I'm happy doing what I'm doing now? This is all I've done, and this is all I know since I got here. If it's in my power I would like to change my fate, so that things don't have to be this way, replied Nene.

What about your former Madam? Did you pay her all the money she said you owe her? Asked Osas. How could I have finished paying 30,000

Euro. That was too much money. I had my issues to sort out including my family. I paid for two years and then quit paying her. She threatened me with the Juju contract and I shrugged it off. She said I'd die if I don't finish paying her remaining money. But I paid half of that then started working for myself. She set me up with a couple of bad guys who threatened me. But I also threatened her that I'll report her to the Police, if she continued harassing me. That was how she stopped troubling me. Now I'm here to lead a freer life. If God wishes, I'll get me a husband here in Germany and then have a family like you. After almost thirty minutes on the phone the conversation ended. But it left Osas with more questions than answers. What a society? You think you're running away from poverty only to end up in another messed up life? "This is sex corruption, point blank practiced in Europe," contemplated Osas. "When would there ever stop the sex tourism in Germany?" They call it Sex Labour? With regular health checks and payment of taxes. Who cares how they coin the name. This is **Sex Corruption** and **Sex Trafficking**, a continued form of **Sex Slavery** lived and endured by these migrants throughout the period of their journey from West Africa. Now it's done in a more conducive and regularized sex industry, exploiting mostly foreign adult migrants knowing it's difficult for them to integrate into their new society. It exploits weak girls and adults who've suffered from sex trafficking and could have had a better chance at integrating into the rest of the society, if not for Germany legalizing another form of sexual abuse, furthering the violence and trauma lived by many young women like Nene. The sad aspect is that, they feed this corrupt and immoral industry from the back and health of innocent foreign girls, who are migrants and refugees, whom study shows that more of them may have been actually trafficked at one time or another, maybe fired from work, unable to fit in socially, and are only continuing a trade they only know how to do.

CHAPTER THREE

AFRICAN AND MIDDLE EAST CRISIS

The migration coming from mostly sub-Saharan West Africa, North Africa and Middle Eastern countries into the European Union in recent years, a situation that has become a focal point for world discussion and controversy, stirring up bitter politics into depths and heights we have not seen for a long time or ever, is in part, due to the flow of resilient people defying violence, persecution and death coming from poor and crisis ridden countries to wealthier nations in Europe and America. It's an unfortunate situation even when the United Nations High Commissioner for Refugees Antonio Guterres now 'Secretary General of the United Nations' declared in a statement in 2015 that the "World stability is falling apart leaving a wake of displacement on an unprecedented scale. Global powers have become either passive observers or distant players in the conflicts driving so many innocent civilians from their homes." Citing conflicts zones in Syria, Iraq, Afghanistan, Somalia, Nigeria, South Sudan, and later Yemen, etc. True, but what about world poverty, unemployment and economic inequality. Yes, the socioeconomic situation of the world has improved in ways it has never been from time immemorial, but many people not limited to Africa and South America are increasingly living in poverty.

If there would be any such concept thought of as 'Third World War' suspected by some conspiracy theorists and mainstream political analysts to be ignited by the world's super power nations as a result of the unnecessary political tensions they create, one might believe is already occurring but not in ways we had imagined it to happen. If there's anything that causes youth restiveness, social unrest, agitation and a degeneration in the moral fabric of any given society and populace of any nation is a situation whereby its people are suffering economically as the same people under those communities are denied equitable distribution of resources and basic social amenities including portable water, housing and means to buy food. It could force such a people to rise in protest to demand a change in government or governance and if that demand is not adhered to, then comes division, crisis, factions rising as separatists and militants in protest as freedom fighters, and eventually such a country degenerates to a full-scale war. If that does not resemble anything we have seen in recent times, then whoever is looking is not really looking at the right place or critical in their holistic examination of the situation.

This situation has occurred over and over and that has led to rise of freedom fighters and terrorists organizations in the places I mentioned earlier such as the oil rich southern and Boko Haram in Northern Nigeria, and has caused the Arab spring protests and wars in places such as Syria that has ultimately destroyed more than eighty percent of the country unleashing a major refugee crisis since world war two, and left its remains shared and distributed among today's world powers, who are fighting proxy wars, worsening situations that are already bad. It's crazy for anyone in Europe or the United Nations to think the world is better-of now than it was in the period after the second world war. The world should keep it hands crossed and hope that this situation as we presently see heightened by the 'America First', 'Nationalism' mistaken for war against globalism and 'Protectionism' antics of America's Trump does not degenerate further or escalate into tensions that will ultimately usher an economic doldrums scenario of a global consequence. Not referring to an earth's invasion or a situation similar to the first or world war but even worse because more people would be affected as opposed to the last wars that affected mostly Europe. Imagine Africa alone is about 1.2 billion people. Fifty percent of that number live in poverty put mildly and not adding abject to it. That would mean about six hundred million people especially in sub-Saharan Africa at least are suffering from one form or level of poverty or the other. These people are estimated to be living under 1.25 Dollar a day.

In a continent that lacks basic social security and welfare system, this would mean such people may not be able to cater their families properly or afford their children's school fees neither provide clothing, housing over their heads and well-nourished food for their children. Moreover, the more children such a family has, the more the situation worsen as that would mean more mouths to feed or provide for. Today, there are few of those poor people coming to Europe on yearly basis to seek a better life, and those European governments are already complaining and using it as a political populist tool to further their agenda to win elections or govern their countries by promoting protectionism and racial nationalism. Imagine when the situation is worse than that and like what I described earlier assume another dimension plaguing Africa and then it eventually leads to crisis and wars. Even though not a full scale one, a factional dissent is enough to descend the nation into a mess like what is happening in recent years in Venezuela or Yemen. Yemeni was a weak state plagued by high levels of poverty, poor economic infrastructure, corruption and terrorism until Saudi Arabian backed coalition in 2015 destroyed what was left of the country after the Houthi rebels forced Yemen's President Rabbu Mansour Hadi into exile. Sometimes, I wonder why that war is not really broad casted or the killings and hunger going on there not brought to the forefront of the media audience.

It's a shame to the world media who chose what to show to the people or not. Imagine in this day and age where television is everything to every home. Why chose to broadcast what they want, or what's interesting, entertaining, magical or what gives the Media stations ratings than what really affect the lives of people. It's true the media focus on the Syrian conflict made the rest of the world to have compassion which led to their neighbours opening up doors to resettle the millions fleeing the crisis including Europe as well as the United Nations expanded capacity to offer aid including temporary shelters, food and education to the young people. Also, the coverage of the news regarding over 200 abducted girls by Boko Haram in 2014 prompting a worldwide outrage while creating awareness of the situation in Northeast Nigeria that have killed about 20,000 people. Among other major crisis covered by the World Media are the American-led invasion of Afghanistan and Iraq in 2001 and 2003 respectively. However, that 'streaming' engine train has long given way to the modern high-speed train.

In other words, if it doesn't create a hype or buzz, journalists don't risk their lives to go there or cover the situation. "The United Nations described Yemeni war as the world's worst humanitarian crisis. But why is it ignored by the world's media?" Venezuela slips daily deeper into food and humanitarian crisis as thousands of that country's citizens can't afford to feed their families while many more flee on daily basis to Columbia and other neighbouring nations. Where are the images on cable Television to feed the world of what's going on there as well as the need for rich countries and powerful individuals to rally around, remove sanctions and invest in the country's economic sector? Always featuring the tweets storm of Donald Trump, the New democratic authoritarian Emperor of America only empowers him to do more. I personally believe if the media ignores his tirade, rhetoric and rantings, not giving it a face, he might change his ways, because it means then he might not be heard and popular as he wanted to be. That brings us to another question, "what's the true role of the Media?" Or is the narrative, interest and conviction not enough for media houses and journalists to constantly feature and educate the public of some of this disquieting malaise?

Why have Media stations such as CNN, CNBC or BBC (British Broadcasting corporation) as some of the most watched media stations in the world not choose outside America at least four presidents or Prime ministers of Nations in Africa and South America to monitor their activities from the day they are sworn into office to the end of their four- or five-year tenure? If they had thought of and executed such programs, I personally think it will affect the way such leaders make their policies as they would be careful not to incur the wrath of the world's public or other world governments and might govern responsibly implementing solutions that might actually bring change to their people. More than ever, with such constant focus on those chosen four world leaders from the very day they are sworn in to the day they leave power, it might help to bring foreign investments to such nations. And finally, it might bring unbelievable change and prosperity to its people including tourism of what those nations got to offer to their people and the world. Once again, the Media stations especially the popular ones are not living up to their full potentials, I can assure you that. But that can change if they are not self-centered on America. The world does not begin and end in America neither Europe nor China, which we see rising today thanks in part to their meticulousness in striving to work hard to bring their people out of the doldrums of poverty and ignorance to the light and real power of economic empowerment to the every day people of that nation. Today, most of the world have in part been taken out of the red zone of poverty due to long term vision and hard work of that country without self-centeredness like what we see in America.

Why would a country's leader tell a company and an entity of world's development in his country not to go outside of his shores to invest in other nations and yet he is in full support of that same company exporting their manufactured goods or products to the rest of the world. How could America call itself a super power nation or the most powerful country in the universe, as some call it, (not minding that there maybe other advanced civilizations in outer space), when they can't export a part of the goodies including creative resources and innovative power from that country to other many poorer nations. What about America's neighbour Mexico? If America wasn't so egocentric, selfish and self serving, how come only that nation grew throughout the twentieth century without positively impacting its neighbours. I bet if Mexico, was the 51st state of America, it could have grown like Los Angeles or New York. When has the world got to this all time low? It is really disturbing. And yet the same America's Trump expects countries in his southern front such as Mexico,

Honduras, Guatemala not to send their people to America to make and have a good life. If the most powerful country on earth stops its industries and companies from going outside its shores to invest especially in poorer countries which it is entitled to or, so we assume, in order to ensure such countries economies are viable and grow in ways that would empower its people to pride and prosperity. The result of those American protectionist and populist propaganda policies, if sustained would eventually do the opposite of what it was trying to avoid, by bringing streams of poor, distraught and beleaguered people bedeviled by violence, wars and poverty.

The worst situation is when those not so well thought out policies harvested from the America's Trump primaries or elections seasons are brought to bear and implemented by the government of the day and supported by the well independent established institutions of that country like its Supreme Court. A case in point was the recent upholding of the policy of American President Trump, a rhetoric echoes from the time of elections where he asked that all Muslims be stopped from coming to his country. Though, due to how unpopular those policies where they were eventually scaled back but still preventing a number of countries including its worst enemy Iran and others such as Yemen, Somalia, Chad, Libya, Syria from coming to his country. Come to think of it, those countries are mostly Muslim countries. But I also wonder why just those countries and not including Saudi Arabia to the list. "Is it done out of prejudice or enmity to send a strong message to those countries on the list?" And why is Saudi Arabia not part of the list? Is it because it's an oil rich country and invests in America? If in case they are trying to prevent terrorists from coming to America to bomb it, according to statistics, most of the terrorists that brought the World Trade Center down and launching attack on America on 911–2001 were mostly Saudi Arabian citizens in America. The ones more likely and with the resources to carry out another kind of terrorism on that scale may not come from any of those countries which the American President and the country's Supreme Court has legally stopped from coming to the United States but from the rich Gulf states. The question now is, what's next? Probably impose more economic sanctions to those poor African nations as part of the list? Could that Travel Ban or other 'America First Protectionism' policies be the answer to America and the world's political and economic problems?

Come to think of it, it's not only Africa that are dealing with this situation of poverty. Greece and Italy in the European Union which are ports of reception of most migrants fleeing mostly poverty, persecution and violence, are not entirely self sufficient. You have many Italians who fled that country in the fifties and sixties into the United States, a place several of them eventually started off or joined illegal businesses or got involved into the opium and drug trade, as several of them eventually became drug lords and kingpins who peddled illicit drug trade from Columbia to the United States, fostering partnerships to create a demand and supply chain, that may be now destroyed in the united States but had lingered on and bedeviled other states in South America even up to this day as the demand never stops.

Even, today several Italian citizens flee their country to other countries in the European Union that are economically viable and each year they move there in droves to secure a good education and good jobs or opportunity such as in Germany and the United Kingdom. The country may be the fourth largest economy in the Euro Zone, but it has many problems besieging its population including lack of adequate or proper opportunities in employment. The same problem that affects many migrants in that country en-route inland Europe, therefore informing why new arrivals into their country would flee to other countries like Sweden or Germany just like its own citizens in order to have a good life. The previous administrations may have recognized these shortcomings and depression in the state of their economic affairs that's why they encourage migrants to go wherever they want to go to. They are not liable to remain in Italy because they know apart from Italy and Greece bearing the brunt of the migration burdened effects, they are just not viable economically to shoulder the responsibility that has fallen on their feet. If there's any country that is presently agitating for a review in the Dublin convention governing migrants settling in their first point of entry is this country Italy because they know it's just too much for them to deal with it saddled with a domestic ruffled economy that even just recently like Spain, Portugal and Greece recovered from economic crisis or are still trying to. But it's not just Italy, it's many of the countries in the Eastern European front including Ukraine, Bulgaria, Slovakia and Romania or the Balkan region.

The Romanians, Bulgarians, Polish and other Eastern Europeans are everywhere in the European Union especially in Germany in recent times. And why would a European country have its citizens fleeing at a massive rate if not for fear of poverty and economic distress they're thrown into. They are no wars in those countries, not at all. But their people flee to other nations where they could secure a better future for themselves and their families. In essence, if one was to calculate the common ratio or denomination for poverty in European standards in those nations and many others across Europe, we'll realize that more than half of all Europeans live in relative Poverty. Knowing this, why would such international bodies most of which are based in Europe be asking migrants to give better reasons for coming into their countries such as Persecutions, political torture or religious violence or war, or what ever reasons stated in the Dublin Convention of why receiving countries should grant stay visas to migrants and refugees, when they know fully well that underlying all those reasons are the fear of poverty, disease and ultimate death.

Whether in war or after war, the reasons people flee from their countries after a major disaster is not unconnected with famine and poverty. Because it takes a long time after a major war, strain or catastrophe that bedeviled a fragile nation for such a nation to recover after that. So, its citizens ultimately find better places or countries where they will lead better lives until things get better in their countries of origin. But even if things do get better, the chances or probability of getting jobs in a country that was once torn by war and is now recovering is less likely, and that might make those who had left to remain in those foreign lands to ultimately become immigrants who might contribute to their destination countries just as it has happened in the past in America and Europe. This situation happened in Germany after the second world war ended as many who left Germany to the Soviet Union or United States never returned. Their next generations in those countries are probably the ones helping those countries especially America in creativity and innovative technology to move that nation to the next level. Europe has spent a better part of the last thousand years fighting wars, and if there's any region of the world that understands migration is Europe. The reason for Portugal and ultimately other past world powers of the 16th to 20th century to set out to discover new worlds were based on this fact of migration due to the constant tensions, stress, agitation, intolerance and wars that besieged Europe. America was established by European immigrants or by slaves who were, on the other hand not voluntary migrants but were forced into slavery to that country to help to establish the New world of America.

That's why when President Trump call Africa and Haiti shit hole countries, I think, he probably doesn't know the history of America.

Like one young African man Joked, "you American people that came and uprooted our ancestral forefathers, don't you know when the time comes their generations in the future or children would go looking for them, at the place you took them to?" He was referring to the American Embassy in Nigeria that refused granting him a visa to travel. It's funny but it's true. Africa built America. They didn't have a choice. Under pain, lynching and extreme violence meted against them, they toiled, and America was ultimately built on their backs. Moreover, it was their huge presence there in that land, that made the Europeans comfortable enough to ultimately move over there in droves to settle and form communities and ultimately govern the land. So, once again, our world was established on the back of migration whether forced, trafficked or voluntary, and we as civilized world today have a duty to protect the unity and development that have arisen from that history of the whole world intermingling, blending and supporting each other to work to enhance the state of the earth. The world is beautiful when it is together and existing as a united entity than when divided. I remember when the Syrians came en-mass into Germany in 2015, some people protested and when some were asked why they didn't like the idea of foreigners coming into their country, they replied because they'll mesh with their white population, conjugate with their women and men to produce mixed babies. That idea of the blood of Germans coalescing with a foreigner like those of Syrians who came into their country in hundreds of thousands, made them against the idea of the German Chancellor welcoming Syrians and other nationalities from Middle East and Africa to Germany.

Is that not a racist idea or a propaganda and agenda for a racist government or state? Was that not the policy of the Nazi Germany, part of the reason that birth the second world war? The idea that Germany led by Nazi government with racial nationalistic views were better than other ethnic tribes and nationalities in Europe, or raising a people that were unique and different, or think they were, from other nations including some in Europe, was not unconnected to why the German Fuhrer, Adolph Hitler tried to conquer the world, while projecting its nation as the noblest state with superior beings of the earth.

So, once again, whether those Hitler sympathizers or Neo-Nazis exist which they do and are expanding at a rapid rate. The spread of their hate ideals should not be the reason why other people in the country must subscribe to their ideology or beliefs, thinking their country was being invaded or overrun by illegal aliens. Who is illegal? And who is not? We are all children and inhabitants of the border less world or earth, given us, in order to make it better for ourselves and for the future generations. Our work as nationals of any country is to ensure we spread the beautiful ideals of love, diversity, peace and unity to all and show it to all. Because today, your country may be on top, who knows tomorrow? You may not be, and the other that is ahead of you would be expected to do the same to you, when you once found it difficult to do the same or show such graceful gesture to them or people of their country when they were knocking at your door for help and support. Emphasizing on the hypothesis of being unique in identity or better of than others based on their skin color has been the basis of bigotry, discrimination, hate and political crisis not just in countries in the Western world or reflected in their colonial policies but also in recent times among social circles and mostly of the cyber propaganda and fake news spreading Internet based social media.

Why should any group of people from any particular country no matter how highly regarded, regard other people who don't look like them to be inferior to them with stereo types positing those people or groups of people from a different continent to being inferior in complex and intelligence. The question of Race and Intelligent Quotient have dominated the internet in recent years, eliciting that sub-Saharan I.Q. is 70 compared to Asians and Whites at 100-110. This in their opinion it means Africa is incapable of producing a civilization like that of America on its own with its enviable strides in science and technology. But those people forget that in the United States, Nigerian educational and income performance index ranks highest overall, even with their supposedly low I.Q.

Racism in Germany is usually associated with far-right groups and Neo Nazis. However, experiences by many foreigners have shown that racism, how be it, subtle, is present in every facet of the society, even in the halls of government. The advertising industry is also guilty of rampant insensitivity towards ethnic minorities. Because the German adverts are funny meant to drain the misery, stress and frustration of the ordinary sad life of a German, some media groups and some of their audience are culpable in this predatory malaise. They think it's perfectly normal to make fun of Blacks or African as well as Asian minority groups.

In television commercials or advert posters Asians and blacks are usually used to either give Germans something to laugh about or they're reduced to ethnic clichés. A case in point could be the racial stereotypical depictions of blacks as victims of war or hunger crisis either always in need of donations or aid to curb poverty or as hip-hop hippies or with certain street cultural hairstyles such as Rastafarian dreadlocks to suit some sexual fantasies or gnawing the sentiments of a depraved outlook. While other clichés not featured in adverts such as hard drugs peddling and usage including crack cocaine, marijuana and opioid is easily captured in the society among social circles and in clubs to be an image born by mostly black or African delinquent youths or criminal adults. Even though this is a disproportionate misrepresentation of the facts and maligning of a certain minority within the community even when research shows that Germans are not only many times more likely to have illegal drug use disorder and abuse but to demand, develop and even peddle especially among the youth population. This makes the viewers to see them as gang criminals, violent, educationally challenged, subservient, ignorant, ugly and grotesque which in turn affects the way the white German population view or treat the greater black population around them especially those of African descent. Also, commercials shown in the German Television that feature black people interested or fantasizing mostly about reggae and sex or the size of their manhood and their citizens seeing them in that light. It may make viewers to laugh but it creates an irreversible impression on the younger generation who view the same people with the same mindset as what they watched on television, making them believe that the black American, Caribbean or African people are good not in any other thing but in hip hop, sex and drugs peddling and are loved only for that purpose.

These social issues elevate us to another important institutional paradigm. Is that not the reason why they are lots of breakups in relationships or marriages among the cultural divide or so they say, in the German population as well as other European countries because they think the Africans or African Americans among them are acclaimed to be only good in at least one vital aspect, sex and their manhood or at least that's how they perceive them to be, and the very day they cease to meet such over-hyped sensational and often exaggerated biased sexual functions or gratify those over sensualized needs, the relationship or supposed love ends automatically. At that time, the authorities will blame it on cultural differences. What stupidity? The same German tourists go to Asia and Africa and would sit and endure unclean environments and would eat the food given them by the locals, even enjoy it better than what they consume in Germany on daily basis. But when they get back and happen to fall in love with those people or immigrants from those nations, they would complain of their food, and state why theirs is better-of.

Many could argue for the reason why, of all the percentage of the Germans marrying or falling in love with an African or African American, why do ultimately out of a hundred percent, about twenty percent or less, are being still married or loving their foreign black or brown partner. If not based on stereotypes, cognitive racism or long effect of such stereo typical forces on their psyche and mindset as a result of the perception rooted in bias manipulations of the broader social truth spread from their local media and American films overtime from when they were young, then tell me what it is? It's simple to understand. They loved the Blackman because of their perception, image fantasy and imaginations of what they think, an affair or sexual relationship with them will look like. In the end, when it turns out not to be what they hoped or envisioned as an absorbing fantasy reality of a sexual experience, the relationship ends even without putting into consideration the overall picture or context and future of their kids, if they are any. They are self-centered and egocentric, all some care about is their self satisfaction and aggrandizement. Soon, is the partnership or relationship fallen out of love, if the African, for example, is granted a legal permanent stay, he goes back home in Africa to remarry a person he or she understands as a partner with similar culture and bring them over to Europe to settle with. That relationship turns out to be long lasting, though not in all cases. Once again, is it a cultural problem, or cultural orientation of Germans, which some could paint as behavioral, which changes are mostly, thrust on them by the information age.

One fresh African immigrant question to a biracial couple was, "why don't you marry this beautiful white girl, instead of going back to Africa to marry a woman and bring to Germany which by the way is very expensive not considering the cost of wedding, court and traditional marriage expenses." Some back in Africa especially the well to do in some societies in Africa are literary coerced to do three marriages. In Nigeria, for example, each of which cost a fortune. But here marrying that girl or lady you amuse yourself with, could cost very little. The responsible answer, the fresh immigrant received, taught him a lesson that in Germany even in Europe as a whole that Nothing lasts forever and so nothing is truly free. The African man in love told him that I always have to be on guard because this girl can fall out of love with me anytime. It's something I can't control. But that trend today isn't only limited to Europe and America alone, as it's spreading to Africa too based on the information and education they get from the public media and films they watch.

"I want it to be that way. But experience has taught me that I can't bet on the future of this romance as is not guaranteed. "We could fall out of love immediately as we fell into it," the guy in love added to the newcomer. It's a delicate thing. Love and relationships are some of the things that have baffled the imagination of some foreigners especially immigrants and migrants into America, United Kingdom, the European Union and Germany, in particular since they came into the country. If you are black or African, they tell you, never befriend or marry a white woman and not be your guard. Always be on alert and put your guard on as a soldier in love because when you think everything is going on well, even when he or she had assured you of the same, you might be surprised to see them do something else such as telling you, 'darling, I don't love you anymore.' Then you'll be left floundering of what you have done wrong.

The truth is, you have not done anything wrong as a migrant or immigrant in this foreign white societies. Some say, you may not be fitting in socially, so it was your doing. No, not at all. You're a victim of a spoiled, self-gratification seeking, over-pampered and ever unfulfilled society and ever emerging societal lifestyles with changing sexual preferences without commitment shaped by television and social media. A situation where men and women fit in only when its suits them and when things don't go their way, they call off the relationship or end the marriage as if it's an on/off switch, sandwich or Pizza order in the middle of the night when hungry for it. The truth about this situation is that, it doesn't only happen to foreigners but to their own people. Sometimes, I wonder why Germans would abandon all this beautiful men and women to go far away to such places as Thailand or Vietnam or South East Asian countries even Eastern Europe to marry a wife or husband. This happen to mostly the men. It's the frustration they face which is not entirely the fault of the opposite partner, as both are culprits or at faults, in this bumpy, wavering, jolting and jumpy man woman relationship situation or ride. No one wants to labour anymore. No one wants to tolerate or support each other to grow mentally and morally while learning to know and understand one another. Parts of the blame lies in the government and social institutions that are not doing enough to promote awareness or educate couples and partners on the essence of stability in partnerships or relationships. A situation expected to go worse in the coming decades. "How come Germans and countries, the world over, teach everything in school but that aspect which is critical to the societal mental and emotional stability, is ignored, and young people are left to make mistakes on their own?"

These days you open the Internet or Television, you hear the same things talked about as those modern forms of technological communication lend a hand to bringing the state of marriage unions and relationships to this point. Some say, during the time of our parents, they would still love themselves. But have they paused to ask themselves why it's no longer the same, and why more and more people are being alone, isolated, socially, emotionally excluded and would rather communicate to their devices than with their fellow humans.

The level of intolerance or lack of strong solid cohesive structure holding up the bond of love of couples and family in the society has reached a peak not seen ever in history and should be given attention or addressed using the same instruments at our disposal, because if it continues this way as priorities and preferences changes and people geared more towards separation, isolationism and independence, then the future might be unsettling. The same changes prone young people to apathy including terrorism being apart from each other sexes and aloof from the rest of the society. Daily the world strangely pushes further the boundaries and conditions towards vain liberal freedom and polarization which doesn't just limit to the friction observed within the environment and stability in sexual relationships and marriages but across the spectrum of all human endeavors. According to an American pew research: "The share of adults who are unpartnered has increased across the young and middle-aged, but the rise has been most pronounced among young adults. Roughly, six-in-ten adults younger than 35 years or 61 % are now living without a spouse or partner, up from 56 % just 10 years ago." Still as part of the pew research, 58 % of all unpartnered adults have never been married. About a fifth of unpartnered adults or 21 % are divorced, 14 % are widowed, and the remainder are either separated or married without a spouse present in the household. While citing education and income as the major factors, it also advocates for social awareness campaigns by government and social institutions. In Germany calls grow for the government to follow the example of the United Kingdom and combat rising cases of loneliness and isolationism. Christian Democrat family's spokesman Marcus Weinberg called for a removal of taboos on the subject so that lonely people have a voice and loneliness doesn't remain a dirty issue. Weinberg argued that the social and health consequences of loneliness would become increasingly important in the coming years. "We have to address the issue by promoting research, launching initiatives and developing new concepts," he said. Bringing lonely people back into communal society is a task that cannot simply be left to commercial providers such as Facebook or dating agencies, he added. Survey shows that 90 % of Germans of varying demographics see loneliness and social exclusion as a problem.

Apart from indigenous Germans, loneliness and isolation are feelings almost every immigrant or refugee is familiar with. The cultural difference between Africa and Middle East, for example and Germany can be shocking, especially for people from smaller towns or communities in Africa whose cultural divide is starkly different with that of Europe, and when they arrive they become disconnected from the social life of the new society and might even take an immigrant years in a foreign land to get used to the culture including how to blend in and interact with people of opposite sexes or belong to social groups. Some never settle in fully. Even if a person has friends or a partner in Germany, for example, when something goes wrong, and the person is broken hearted or suicide prone, not having family around during those times can make things even harder. Family is a support system, some take for granted at home, with a father, mother, brother, sister and uncle or aunt close by.

Once again, it takes us to the grim hole of intolerance, as that sentiment stretches beyond not liking a foreigner but to every other aspect of the human family life. It will take humanity or people whether in Europe, Asia or America time to step backwards and reflect, as their inability to resolve their differences peacefully and coexist, shatters the very fabric of our morals and values of unity and love even amongst families or folks. I always wonder why African countries and other Asian nations such as China and Japan are not open to continental migration like Europe, even though it's what's needed to make their societies diverse, young and immigrant skilled labour intensive and technology friendly to take them to the next level. For Africa, it will help them to diversify not only their population but their economy, to make the continent attractive and an ordinary westerner eying Africa less afraid to live and raise a family in that society. The failure of African countries to grow and expand by setting in motion deliberate approaches to open up their borders to the world, contemplate on racial diversity, strategize policies to lure not only experts but ordinary westerner looking for elsewhere to live, and to integrate themselves into the future of Africa and contribute to managing the production and distribution flow of goods and services to evenly affect all is probably rooted in this same reasons of ignorance, apathy and egocentricity of them not opened to migration or welcoming immigrants from other races and cultures to live and coexist with their people. When a traditional Japanese, Chinese or east Asian ethnicity even Indians consider their own people, blood and race to be pure, unadulterated and not customarily inclined to transcultural marriages to further their lineage and capacity of their future generations to grow in intelligence and body symmetry or look, it will come to a time when, their elasticity will stretch itself hitting a dead end. When that happens without no other way to navigate itself out of the situation unless it starts opening up the door and being receptive as well as interactive with other races and people of different cultural backgrounds and diversity and accepting them as fellow human beings including loving their own minority communities that embraces a multicultural identity, then, it will get stalled to the past.

In the United States, according to recent survey whites account for under Half of all Births in that country, in some States. This includes Japanese and Chinese making up that estimate. Such a turn has been long expected but no one knew the moment it would arrive in a country that was dominated by white Europeans and has battled with issues of racism throughout the period of the civil war to the civil right era and recently with debates to restrict immigration under Donald Trump. While all over the world whites including Europe and Asia will remain a majority for some time. We should have it in mind that a younger generation is being born in a minority that will one day emerge a majority with broader implications for the world's identity, economy and political life. The world is fast desegregating itself into a detribalized, united and interactive global and multi-ethnic organism, and might end up in the future becoming a mixed racial entity in less than two hundred years. But scientific thinkers, believe ultimately human beings around the Earth would all go Black, in at least a thousand years from now. This is because of the dominant genes or genome of the 'dark skinned' African locked hidden in the DNA of every person born on Earth.

Just like South Korea that has a three percent rate of accepting and integrating asylum seekers, Japan don't really welcome immigrants neither grant asylum to foreign migrants. According to official records Japan took in just 28 refugees in 2016, despite record applications of over ten thousand people. In 2017, Japan accepted 20 out of 20,000 applications. Immigration is a controversial subject in Japan, where many prides in the purity of ethnic homogeneity despite the shrinking workforce and aging population. Yet millions of those Japanese are every where from America to Europe. Maybe it's because their economy is good and by accepting other people from other Asian nations, Africa and even Europe in large numbers into their land to settle might put a strain on their economy. Actually, if they do it will improve it in the long run. Every system and area of that country might become diverse and better of. This also applies to all countries including Africa and Middle East. If they only learn to integrate and tolerate other cultures and people from elsewhere and to interact with them, marry, work with, and allow to settle in their countries. What is it with culture anywhere? "Are our individual cultures more important than the basic freedom of human beings to life and movement or showing love to other people in need?"

Recently, the local Muslim Rohingya population of Myanmar, after years of discrimination and persecution, were finally driven away from their homes, while their communities were burnt, as they fled to the neighbouring country Bangladesh to find refuge. Over 500,000 people were displaced as the United Nations in 2017, called it the "World's fastest developing refugee emergency and a humanitarian and human rights nightmare." Adding that the humanitarian crisis is a breeding ground for radicalization, criminals and traffickers. The broader crisis has a degenerative multiple implication, including risk of inter-communal strife. What stops Japan from taking in and integrating a few thousands of those suffering refugees into their country? It sounds simple, but that might be the last thing they would want to do. Again, based on that behavior from the Asian powers like South Korea, Japan and China, one will view the European nations as God sent or Angels when it comes to these aspects of humanity and soul in the face of agony, despair and suffering faced by poor refugees and migrants despite the simmering tensions for a radical change in the way they do things now more than ever before even as right wing anti-immigration racists groups and populist governments have taken over the business of the day including the seat of power in some of this European Union countries in order to change things or reverse course to status quo. In China Hubei provincial exhibition, titled; "This Is Africa" was a display of gallery images featuring Africans and animals together. The Museum exhibition in October 2017, had elephants, cheetahs and lions alongside the wild faces of Africans, with one section of the exhibition, titled; "One's mind tells their appearance." It was eventually brought down due to complaints. Imagine, irrespective of the collaboration between China and Africa, there's not enough sensitization on the subject of racism.

Could those racial, religious and ethnic sentiments as well as pride in ethnic homogeneity seen upheld in Japan, South Korea or China, be the reason they hardly open their doors to migration or grant permanent stay status to Migrants and Refugees hoping for the time when peace would return in those troubled lands for their people to return back? If that is the case, then it's even worse. But unfortunately, that is what is happening all over Europe right now. Saying to themselves, *"let us let them in, when it's time, we will throw them all out."* If it's so then, then it's actually pitiful and we have not learned anything. Are the European countries just faking their humanity to the suffering migrants coming to Europe? Come to think of it, apart from the Syrians who earlier on in 2015 and 2016 were granted a residence status in Germany and Sweden, I mean the early arrivals, other countries migrants and refugees including Africa and the other middle east migrant foreigners or asylum seekers in the European Union cries out to them for mercy but are largely ignored. In Germany, the very thought of granting their residence status to illegal aliens doesn't please the elite, including those in the country's national Parliament called the 'Bundestag' who makes and changes migrations laws regularly to the detriment of migrants and refugees, as some share a common feeling and thoughts with the hardliners of being either betrayed by their Chancellor, invaded by adversaries or dancing to the tune of a detestable song. Either way, the entire episode of events is viewed as unthinkable and frowned at. Again, I might be wrong, but I think like the neo-Nazi groups including PEGIDA in the streets of Eastern Germany, there are several lawmakers in the nation's parliament who are racists, bigots and haters not limited to those on the right-wing anti-immigrant parties. The very idea of their country accepting and integrating migrants or taking in many asylum seekers, to them is unimaginable. The idea of seeing all those presently stationed in their country though rejected asylum ultimately gaining a stay to being here much longer is even torturous, irrational and intolerable.

One might classify the administration of the Germany's Chancellor as moderate, liberal, progressive and different from those in other parties whose views are on the extreme right or left as she is one of the few right thinking heads among many bitten or wounded people waiting for her to leave office to be able to implement their racists ideas as policies for the desperate populace who wanted change. Election periods are often the right times to further their agenda by manipulating the minds of the people to think the problem of the country is caused by immigrants and refugees, and the only way their country will return to peaceful and orderly manner is for the migrants and refugees to be stopped completely from coming to their countries and secondly, deport all those who are in their country, which are most, because they hardly give a permanent residence stay status to migrants from West Africa, Middle East and elsewhere these days, or ever. Once again, it's a problem affecting everyone. I mean, it's not a problem but they choose to make it one. Europe and Germany would rather choose to invest in America, and not Africa, the country that is coming back to bite them in 2018 by standing against their policies of free trade and transatlantic shared ideals, because to them that continent is not economically viable.

Imagine, since 2015 mass migration into Europe, if some of these economically viable European countries had entered Africa and wanted to make a difference in those nations, they could have made strides by now. But No, they would choose to bicker about Africa and their corruption and make friends with rich America, a world power instead. Why don't they groom other world powers to their level, to enable them to trade and compete with them effectively. More than ever, to have a choice to foster trade with Africa and the middle east viably, if America turns their back on them like it's happening now. Sometimes, one might wonder what the European representatives discuss about while in Brussels European parliament. Perhaps, they discuss it but no follow up compelling commitment. Even, when those commitments are held, and trade agreements are made, it's mostly unfair and unbalanced, and made for the benefit of the European Union as their capacity to produce, innovate and export, far outstrips and outlasts that of many countries in Africa. As long as others are hungry or persecuted or in war or violence, Europe may never be able to stop migration or have peace on that matter unless they decide to look the other way, if they see migrants in the high seas struggling to survive and reach Europe, which is also an option.

Maybe, one day, they might be able to look into the situation carefully and correct it as opposed to the way immigration and politics in the Euro Zone is progressing right now. If charity or non-governmental organizations carry suffering migrants from the sea and no country decides to take them in, then it might make the aid agencies to think twice and may be next time, may not go up to the sea to look for and help save fleeing migrants and refugees in a risky situation. Why would countries, above all things, not think about the only thing that might help to stop the migration, which is undoubtedly economic investments in Africa, educational and vocational training, withdrawing sanctions and making peace among warring parties, tribes, ethnic groups or militant groups in the middle east, Africa or any other part of the world. It appears difficult until it's done. If America or Europe are actually interested in making peace among the various world fighting factions, they could. These people who are fighting for freedom or terrorists are people too, and at the end of the day, all of them want peace and prosperity. Don't forget, these conflicts thrive in mostly poor countries. This means there's a relative equation to why they persist or continue in their freedom fighting or terrorists' actions. In countries, where there's corruption, poverty and an unfair or unequal state of distribution of the means of production and distribution among its population, issues such as these arises and thrives in that environment. Or put differently, when there is the inability for the country to rise above poverty to provide for its people, the only way for those groups to survive is to strife or perpetrate their crimes. Most of these separatists or freedom fighters are not interested much in attacking and bombing their people and neither was their initial ideology tailored in this manner. If only International Peace organizations wouldn't give up on them as a result of their brutality and keep pushing on to broker peace among and between the separatists and the government, no matter how blacklisted they are, I believe they have ears to hear and mind to think, and when the terms favour them, they might ultimately change their ways, disband their terror groups and follow another path which benefits the entire country. Just like the Niger Delta militants, Boko Haram of Northeast Nigeria, Yemeni Houthi rebels, Somalia Al-Shabaab or ISIS in Syria and Iraq, Taliban in Afghanistan and Pakistan, etc., if we stop to bedevil them and reason with them using negotiating parties, to look into their plight and promise to meet them, which will primarily be economic, social or equal chance to play a role in their political governance, peace would reign around the world. Especially, if those terms reached are met, by the super powers of the world, committing their resources and devotion to improving the socioeconomic state of those countries, then the ultimate result will be peace cemented on fertile grounds, that would only continue to grow. Not standing afar and poking sharp fingers to the situation, by blaming the factions, people and leaders for their failure or situation their country has fallen into, instead of stepping in to show them how things are done, for the local population to be able to stand up and manage their resources both human and material effectively with the economic support framework and trade with other world leading nations, will ultimately make a great difference.

Back to the countries of source of migration and their democratic leadership that is anything but stable, and as a result, of the bleak economic prospects of its people and future, many people exit their countries of birth to make a new life elsewhere, the wealthier nations can actively play a role to change that situation, so that it doesn't continue unabated. There's no reason why Nigeria, Ethiopian, Ghana, Pakistan and Iraq can't strive to be South Korea or China. With the right framework and intelligent support of other technological nations and diplomacy, Africa could rise to fulfill its purpose to its people and stand as a shinning light for future to come. It's time for wastefulness, corruption, recession, retrogression and moral degradation of Africa and the world to end. The blame laying on all sides whether the economically prosperous nations, middle income or the poorer countries, it's all our business to ensure all countries and individuals are economically free and independent.

For many years people have talked about corruption being the cause of why Africa is largely poor from West to East Africa even to the Southern part of the continent. According to transparency international, corruption is prevalent in almost every country in the world, but some are more corrupt than others. But the question is, "why are some corrupt and are still progressing while others mostly in Africa don't?" The corruption didn't stop those richer countries in South East Asia, East Asia and Middle East, Europe even America from being creative, socially vibrant or progressing scientifically and technologically. That is largely due to the fact that those countries' socio economic and political institutions including Democracy, rule of law or justice system, government bureaucracy, health, private property rights and financial markets as well as incomes, gender equality, social norms are well developed and strengthened. Another advantage to them is because they have the right tools and infrastructure to continually improve and invite the best minds into their nations in order to grow and expand. On the other hand, what do African leaders do? They are stuck with the discourse of the politics of tribalism, ethnicity and religion including favoritism and nepotism, an obstacle to their political stability, wealth creation, growth and progress, which they're unable to overcome. That is the cause of corruption and depression in some African countries and the leading cause of why nations such as oil-rich Nigeria, Kenya, Ghana, South

Africa, Egypt fails to rise to fulfill its potentials and promise to its people despite its abundant God given resources and well-read population within and outside the country.

A case in point is Nigeria. Why should a democratically elected head of state or a state Governor be overcome by nepotism, favoritism and tribalism, as that politically elected leader would leave an entire city full of millions of people, but will devote resources to, and implement a major project in his small village or community even when he knows that there lie no capacity whatsoever for such a national project to survive there due to lack of education, poverty, access to basic services and a fewer population who are mostly young and old people. On the other hand, if such a large project was placed in a bigger city that could support the population and the larger population in turn supports the project investment in terms of patronizing it to grow, eventually such a business organization or corporation will thrive and go back to invest in those smaller communities with the immense support and investments it gets from the larger city. It makes a good economic sense. Or why would a federal minister give federal contracts to people because such people come from his or her village, city or state and speak his language even though he knows those people might not harness the means to ensure such a huge project is effectively executed. The one with the means and right ideas or technology on how to make sure such a project is executed with the vision of development and sustainability is ignored or never made to qualify for such federal contracts. This ugly situation rooted in age-old ethnic and religious prejudice enthroning half baked amnesia struck corrupt politicians as democratic leaders with organizing principles based on nepotism and misogyny is part of the problem of under development and cause of several crises in Nigeria and Africa.

A country where a President or Governor steals from the treasury to only develop his community or save to serve only his tribal people or family, while those in other communities and towns are left to wander why the benefits of democracy is not extending to them and their communities including building roads, social facilities, power and establishing of companies to access employment opportunities for all to equally benefit from, irrespective of where they come from or what ethnicity or religion in Nigeria, they are of. That is the problem of Nigeria today. Before Democracy gained roots in Nigeria in May 29th, 1999, the country's past military rulers had stolen from the country, and due to sanctions leveled at the country by western powers, and lack of access to technology and economic infrastructures, the country stagnated for decades, as in most situations the proceeds from the oil sales don't always translate to the welfare of its citizens. A situation that made many in the 1980's to migrate en-mass to the United States and the United Kingdom to seek greener pastures.

Today, the country's democratic leader, forgetting that the present state of Nigeria is borne by the domino effect of the past misuse of the country's resources by its past rulers, which President Buhari was part of, and would rather accuse its people of being lazy, that's why they're not productive, tells of the daft, dozy and unintelligent leaders elected to power that govern Africa right now. The same President Buhari ordered about 900,000 agonizing Ghanaian migrant workers and residents due to austerity to leave Nigeria in 1983 and 1985 with an ultimatum, when he first came to power through a military coup, and up until this day, Ghanaians have partial love lost or cognitive behavioral apathy for their fellow Nigerian West Africans, whether consciously or otherwise, due to this very single imperious highhanded policy of Buhari. An event infamously marked by a ridiculous phrase ... "Ghana Must Go." Hope he could one day apologize to them for that grave mistake. The same President of Nigeria, knowing the Northern part of Nigeria where he hails from as mostly Muslims hardly travel out to the western nations, told Angela Merkel and the rest in Europe to send back Nigerian asylum seekers, that nothing is wrong with Nigeria. What would they do if those migrants are returned, eat grass or go into the life of crime where many are doomed to languish in, due to lack of opportunities or strategic approach to resolve the economic and political quack mire. His May 2018 nationwide approval poll ratings by THIS DAY, shows President Buhari stands at about 41 % but under 30 % sounds like closer to the true situation of how people feel in that country.

Like the situation that happened recently in South Africa where the local white minority population farm owners were attacked by some blacks with rising racial tensions and their political leaders stoking fires, who recently asked that some of their lands be expropriated among the local black population, since most of the land of that country is the hands and control of the minority white population even after the fall of Apartheid in 1994. But many dared not to consent to it, saying it's wrong and that they're not giving up their land to any poor black people to own and use them to contribute to the economic growth and empowerment of the poor Africans in that nation. They accused the administration of President Ramaphosa of discriminating against them and virtually targeting and ordering them to be killed by thugs. One would guess, it's simple. If the white population who are mostly in control of all the country's land and economy, come together, meet and agree with the current administration, on how parts of their lands, could be shared to and managed by the black people whom some claim are not creative, while they are compensated as they will also help and support the new black land owners in terms of know how or ideas on how to operate their farms, then the country would not have descended into the poor state it did recently. A situation where Australia had to offer Asylum to White South Africans who were hunted by those same people they once hunted and oppressed while taking everything away from them including their lands, dignity and freedom. "What about the philosophy of live and let's live?" Over seventy percent of the lands, over twenty years after the fall of Apartheid are still controlled by the white population who claim they came into the country at about the time the black people also settled in that land called South Africa, a couple of centuries prior. Like one commentator puts it, the country is suffering from a cycle of oppression, xenophobia, racial discrimination and superiority, a problem that wasn't completely resolved and it was bound to occur.

That's a long history of South Africa to recount. Everyone knows the right thing to do but they don't want to do it. The wealth of South Africa is controlled by the white population even though they make up a fraction of that population due to situations such as still laying claims to large swaths of lands as important means of production while the black majority even their wealthy real estate developers hardly come by any land to develop because most of the lands are controlled by a few. The global community is failing to recognize the inadequacy in the present economic system prevailing in the world. "It's called Equality and Sharing." A system that would one day question, challenge and unseat the current inadequate and cracked ideology of "Democracy." A system that manages a fair distribution of the means of production and wealth to its people. The application of this vital concept of fairness, equality and sharing by the country's rich elite and government friendly policies can help distribute wealth fairly amongst its citizens. Something the system of the world's governments don't understand right now because they're not practicing it or maybe it doesn't favour the aristocratic and capitalistic minded in richer societies, and therefore stereotyped it. If there's the existence of such a concept at all in the dictionary of the world today, they wouldn't be wars, hunger and fighting. As a result of this capitalistic or aristocratic system of economic governance practiced by most parts of the world today, whereby a rich few are as rich as the bottom one hundred percent, freedom fighters take matters into their hands to fight to free themselves and prove the righteousness of their cause.

As long as the present world thrives in an unsustainable liberal capitalism, socialism and communism system of governance, as well as globalization furthering corruption and inequality, a system that take from the poor and give to the rich making the rich few grow even more richer, then, peace in the world will not be sustainable over a long time. Because no matter how many people are involved in commerce and business of trade of demand and supply, without setting up a deliberate and holistic fair system or economic approach in the world that will ensure that the planet is saved and the poor are not left behind in a prosperous or poor state of economy, then, they'll always be poor people on earth and the planet will continue to be depleted. The very thing the world or United Nations' sustainable development goals is trying to address but they can't due to the already established and prevailing false and misleading systems of governance and unjust rule of law around the world that protects them. All people can't trade all the time. Some will work for those who are successful traders or entrepreneurs, and in that situation or market system where greed causing economic depression or inflation drives cost of goods and services to the roofs, the rich are the only ones that benefits, while the common workers and the vulnerable are left at their peril without a raise in salary, social security as well as the poor in the villages lost in time or to the progress of time. Unfortunately, that is the system operated by the world democratic powers today and it will be difficult to exist as a country on earth and practice anything different from that, if not your country might not meet up nor attract the much-needed investments from foreign nations who wants every nation to operate according to their map or guidelines to curry their favour or investments.

The world needs to rethink its whole concept or economic approach to prosperity. *Perhaps, it's time for a new system to emerge from the ashes of the old.* Either way, it's inevitable as forecasting shows that apart from other uncontrollable forces battling this current flawed system that doesn't support development neither sustainable in the long-term, the larger human family will from, on or before

2030 begin to seriously rethink the entire economic approach to prosperity. To avoid a total political, social, environmental and economic collapse, the world needs to move beyond the current standard choices of capitalism and the false system of socialism even communism practiced in the world today. An equitable system of governance even under democracy that would ensure those left behind are carried along and the windfall from the rich are not only transferred to the government coffers but used to drag the poor out of poverty, along with a community social framework for health, education and financial empowerment of the poor, will eventually ensure every country's ideological economic system is sustainable. Moreover, the rich, middle- and poor-income countries will have no poor people in their streets as poverty may further be reduced. That kind of system which is unlikely to be thought of, as long as the Americans control much of the world's economic and financial regulatory system and rather think the 'elitist governing system' of Capitalism and Aristocracy is the real deal, while never imagining another ideology replacing it now or in the future. Africa is caught up in this dilemma of a world controlled by America and China, who claim to be all seeing but are actually blind, despite the height of their technology of the future or civilization.

More than ever, they are followed by Europe who have shown in actions recently that they are nothing but puppets or raging bulldogs without actual teeth to bite. On their part, they are controlled by the authoritarian administration of Trump in America and are unable to make independent decisions to favour any country including Iran which was recently sanctioned by America because of their age-old prejudices against that country and its leadership. Though, Europe is up for all sanctions against that country being lifted especially after the last nuclear deal reached with Iran under President Obama administration. But there's nothing they can do on their own since their countries are all very well invested in America that control and give them the better returns for their investments than other countries. In that situation, America, as the country they benefit from, knowing its power over them, can willingly sanction the companies operating from Europe or whipping them to compliance in line with their policies no matter how opposed they are to such irrational policies.

The former American administration has led and executed a deal to curb Iran from producing Nuclear weapons, a treaty that will see them inspected and monitored while they give up on their ambitions to develop any nuclear weapons, A treaty supported by Europe until 2025. In turn will see them rewarded as billions of dollars will be released to them, and investments allowed to come into that country. But recent happenings have shown that America were not happy about that deal after all. With the New Administration of Trump, that have rejected and shredded that treaty entered between his last administration and Europe calling it weak and inadequate. A situation that saw Iran now cringing and complaining not to do anything else demanded by them from the American president including curtailing their terrorist activities in other nations in the middle east such as Iraq, Syria and Yemen. The European Union, though against the new American policy are unable to change anything because their hands are tied, it's unnerving and straining to the European Union who now see that despite their many differences not least the immigration issue in Europe among its member states, they are faced with having to battle with America's Donald Trump concerning his rash policies which don't augur well for their economies or not in line with their Union policies.

So that's the nature of the present world. In turmoil, partly due to the irrational, absurd and implausible actions taken by America and its leadership. They say it's peaceful, but I say it looks like chaos to me. A time bomb waiting to explode on all front unless addressed on all sides with love, earnest determination and the political will. If not primarily addressed and every country including America seeking only the best for its people without caring about others, sooner or later, the fragile state of peace created among nations after the second world war under international bodies such as the United Nations Organization might burst into flames along with the fire they are trying so hard to quench. The world's bubble is bubbling under a staggered cooling fire of failed diplomacy, but what happens when the cooler or freezer stops cooling or fails to work anymore, then it's evident that the fire under it will be so intense that it will burst the bubble with an explosion that might lead to separation, chaos and interspersion of nations into a dark and strange places that would be very hard though not impossible to come back from. Temporary stress reliever such as the political dramas emanating from Trump tweet tirade and other strongmen rhetoric, will only divert people from the real issues and elongate or prolong the efforts of meeting and working together as one-world to discuss the currents of real issues affecting the world whether in countries where migration is coming from or the nations that are divided on how to manage the migration issues as well as the cause of the problem including hunger, terrorism crisis, inequality, bad governance and corruption leading to division and breakdown of law and order within those countries or regional unions.

Sending migrants or failed asylum seekers back to their homeland which the receiving countries have refused to grant asylum due to a cruel politicized system such as in the European Union that is muddled up in politics of identity, race and economics, is not the solution to the problem. The politics of migration whether legal or not, a situation even which the judiciary are not spared in the quagmire, as they join politicians to rebuke asylum seekers in their courts by outright refusal to grant them a stay status, no matter the vital context of their testimony, only adds to speak to a world that is inhumane, unjust or just don't care. What are the countries in Africa and Middle East doing to change all these? They probably are as confused as Europe and America because if they couldn't serve the millions of people currently living in their own countries effectively and being accountable to them, as well as striving hard to create more opportunities for their people by partnerships with foreign governments and independent bodies to invest in their countries for a capacity for their people to grow, then, it's same old dilemma, it'll create, forcing more migrants and refugees out of their lands to the western world.

I have heard severally how people especially in Europe keep blaming the African countries or its leaders in its failure to provide a better working environment and livable society for its people. It's true, as they criticize, so do the migrants. Imagine, the entire sub-Saharan Africa can hardly boast of sufficient electric power supply to it people. No functioning water department to provide quality water for its people to drink and when needed. There's inflation, a constant increase in the cost of goods and services in the market. Sometimes, one wonder how do Africans who live in these countries survive, especially where financial resources for expenditure are lean or scarce and disposable income is hard to come by? Many Africans who migrated and now live their lives in Europe and America often ask how to do their present countries, which they currently reside in, manage to make things work in their countries, and the same things fail to work or function properly in Sub-Saharan Africa?

Again, it has to do with not just one reason but several including lack of capital, creative ideas and economic infrastructures even basic technology, of how things work. Secondly, poverty. This means even when some of those services such as epileptic power supply or pipe borne water are supposedly functional and serving several cities such as in Nigeria, for example, the consumers find it difficult to meet up with their payments, thereby the government or companies handling or overseeing this services are unable to further the provision of those services, as a result shutting down when no further federal investments come into them. These facilities though are able to work in bigger cities like Lagos or Abuja in Nigeria but the country over the years have suffered from lack of sufficient investments to fund these crucial sectors adequately resulting in individual homes largely providing their own water supply as each house digs its bore-hole, and from it they fill their over head tanks which in turn supply water to the taps in their homes. The country has suffered many setbacks over the years leading to its inability to develop many of its critical sectors that impacts the people including healthcare, power and education.

But since 1999, Nigeria according to economic statistical data has grown steadily until the recession that knocked it down by the end of 2014. The question is, through that 15 years long period, how many lives have been impacted by its gains or democracy and peace, instead what the people saw was the rise of the Niger Delta freedom fighting groups in 2006 springing up demanding equal sharing of resources that emanates from where the oil resources are taken from because they're not positively impacted by it. Lately, was the rise of Boko-Haram in the country from 2009 through 2014, when their notorious reputation came soaring due to their ruthless terrorist activities, and are still active, having killed over 20,000 innocent lives and were responsible for the abduction of the 'Chibok Girls' from their school dormitory in Borno State of Nigeria sparking a global reaction and movement, tagged; 'BRING BACK OUR GIRLS,' on the back of a country that have neglected its people in spite the poverty suffered by many of its people. A terrorist organization that paints itself as a group annexed to ISIS that fights to Islamize the country while campaigning to taking the youths out of education as it considered a taboo before their belief system. One might argue that those belief systems are hatched from the fanatic and stringent Islamic traditions prevalent in this region, the Northern part of Nigeria for a long time. But the truth lies in the fact that the country and its leaders have failed its people over the many years of its rule not only due to corruption but have not put in place the right policies and institutions that will make this ever crooked path straight and plucking its ever growing population out of ignorance and poverty into the light of education, economic empowerment and true freedom.

"If those people that started Boko Haram had jobs or were working in one sector of the country's economy or the other and were educated with a socially secured future, what on earth would make them go and take up guns to terrorize the public threatening the social and political stability and fabric of the society to achieve an aim, a selfish aim at that?" Tell me! These problems facing Nigeria are also the underlying causes of some of the crisis in most African war torn, hungry and poor nations such as the Democratic Republic of Congo, a country that have from the most part since its independence suffered from one form of violence, terror and war, or the other, while most of the population suffered from hunger and abject poverty.

In 2017, the disasters and emergency committee, an alliance of 13 leading British aid agencies raised funds for South Sudan, Somalia, Kenya and Ethiopia which was hit by drought. The United Nations even warned the world could face the largest humanitarian crisis since the end of the second world war. With millions in four countries facing starvation and famine. South Sudan as the world's youngest nation is causing Africa's biggest refugee crisis with three million fleeing their homes due to civil war caused by two opposing power-hungry factions. It was estimated in the same year that more than 100,000 South Sudanese are experiencing famine, with a further one million on the brink of starvation. Almost five million people, more than four in ten people of the country are short of water and food. Aid workers have been unable to reach tens of thousands in need due to war, lack of access at checkpoints and looting of humanitarian compounds.

In war torn Somalia, more than six million people had no access to reliable water and food, and there are additionally 360,000 acutely malnourished children. Experts even warned it could be a repeat of the famine that struck that country in 2011, which killed 260,000 people. This country in the Horn of Africa in the region of Eastern Africa, among Eritrea and Djibouti, has been subject to repetitive cycles of drought and famine. In 2008, United Nations designates Al Shabaab, a militant group in Somalia linked to Al Qaeda, as a foreign terrorist organization. Alongside, a United Nations security Council unanimously votes to allow countries to send war ships into Somalia waters to combat piracy, a situation that has troubled many western nations shipping lines as many were taken hostage with huge ransoms demanded from them to free them, the money which was further used to carry out other terrorists' activities including bombings destroying lives and poverty. It was reported that 16 million people in East Africa were in need and seek help to secure their livelihoods and acquire adequate food. Nine million children needed nutrition assistance. The recurring East Africa drought make it difficult for farmers and herders to produce crops and feed livestock.

While seasonal rains of that year that began in February and March have been plentiful in some places, excessive amounts of rains falling on drought-stricken land has resulted in flash floods, killing more than 300 people and washing away crops and shelters. Children were worst hit with the development of the health and mental faculty impacted. More than 15 Million children in Ethiopia, Kenya, Somalia and South Sudan were struggling to get enough to eat. Floods increased the risk of Cholera and other water borne diseases among people with temporary shelter and poor sanitation or wellbeing. Remember in 1985, Famine in Ethiopia caused by drought in the northern highlands and problems regarding delivering aid led to one million deaths and massive displacements, probably the worst famine in modern history.

During the second Congo war in 1998–2004 more than three million people died in the Democratic Republic of Congo, mainly from starvation and disease. In 2015 to 2016, a strong El Nino affected almost all of East and Southern Africa, causing food insecurity for more than fifty million people. In 2018, from February to May, torrential rains in East Africa caused flood that killed people, livestock and crops, and washed away roads and bridges making it hard to deliver aid. Generally, in Africa, recurring drought, conflicts, terrorism and instability have led to severe food shortages. Many countries in the continent have struggled with extreme food shortages over the years including poverty and the lack of government and community economic and social support systems to help their families, relatives and citizens withstand the impact of this menace. Like in East Africa, a recurring cycle of drought caused the plunging of communities in famine and poverty again before they have the chance to recover from the past one. In South Sudan, many had fled their homes due to the conflicts, and few farmers have been able to harvest a crop. This caused inflation in market prices of goods and agricultural produce.

More also, during the rainy season, much of the country is inaccessible by roads which limits transportation of food aid as well as goods sent to the market for sale. In cases where there are flash floods and overflowing rivers that blights crops and roads, under such condition parents could hardly afford enough food to eat, and eventually they'll need emergency aid from the government agencies and aid groups, when they run out of money and food. The longer these situations persists, the more the people suffer from the effects of lost livelihoods and homes including long-term mental and psychological damage and deaths. The consequence of this incessant occurrence of clashes, war and drought causing famine has led hundreds of thousands of migrants and refugees storming out of the continent to the middle east countries including Saudi Arabia and Israel, places where they are not liked neither wanted including fleeing to Europe and America.

CHAPTER FOUR

GERMAN IMMIGRATION POLICY THROES

Although the German Chancellor Angela Merkel has been seen as a long-time defender of the rights of legal immigrants, migrants and refugees arriving not only in her country but in other countries of Europe including Austria, Hungary, Poland, Greece, Italy and Sweden. Essentially since 2015 she has fought and striven to show the face of European humanity which she said was the 'soul' of the entity but the unsettling rising tide of discrimination and fascism towards Africans and Middle Easterners coming into their borders is tending to create a situation where those in the German party known as Christian Social Union, the Bavarian allies in the Chancellor's team to use this crisis as a reason to further their agenda of divisive politics, hate and bigotry against mostly young men and women who are fleeing war, hunger and persecution. Perhaps, she may want to reconsider the entire approach of a coalition government whether she wants to have these people sitting in her table as her allies who are fighting and resisting her policies and everything she has stood for, at a time the rest of Europe are reneging on such stance, the one she has held dear for some time now. Though, Germany has always faced migration issues and shouldered them due of their political will, financial and most of all, what experience has taught them, but since 2015, the tide has greatly shifted as in the recent years, more pressure has been mounted on her to take a tougher stance to curtail the migrant push towards her borders especially in Bavaria, a German state that have managed the migration properly but also where their stance are increasingly toughened on refugees and migrants. She has been in talks in many occasions not only with her fellow party, allies and opposition member parties but with other world leaders in Europe and

America in order to get an aligned way of how to deal with this crisis, and this time may signal the end of her era, the Merkel era, though not sure, unless she totally plays into their political 'game of thrones.'

Along with the President of France Emmanuel Macron, they are seen as the last Bastions of free movement not only among or within the European Union to counter the recent United Kingdom's vote to secede from the greater European union for issues such as Migration of not just foreign migrants coming across the sea but also within the European Union. Therefore, she is seen as the last defender of the European liberal democracy amid the rise of populism across the Continent. Merkel, although not clear may be forced to make a U-turn on her open-door policy which has already been scaled back since Germany opened its borders to welcome around a million asylum seekers in 2015, which had according to estimates ten thousand people arrived daily in a population of eighty-two million people.

Her lenient refugee policy is blamed for a surge in support of the far right 'Alternative for Germany's rise, which became the main opposition party after 2017 September inconclusive elections. Germany's political turmoil came amid a rise in populism and anti immigration sentiments across Europe including its neighbours such as Poland, Austria and Hungary. The resurgence in far-right sentiments leaves Germany's political elite now in disarray as the opposition voice gets the stronger. Austrian Chancellor Sebastian Kurz, a leader of that country that came to power amid a rise in populism, a conservative critic of Merkel policy for migration, has recently pushed for 'Axis of the Willing' among Austria, Germany and Italy to fight illegal migration, as they call it. It is a view shared by German Interior Minister Horst Seehofer, who has vowed to reject migrants at his country's border, if they have already registered in European Union States to the South. In March 2018 Seehofer told a Newspaper that *"Islam doesn't belong to Germany."* He is a member of the Christian Social Union, Bavarian allies of Angela Merkel who are further to the right than her own Christian Democrats (CDU). He clearly indicated his intentions to execute a "Masterplan for Quicker Deportations." It is a mutiny led by her internal affairs minister, a move at least 62 % of German citizens were against. It is feared that the fragile coalition, his party has with Angela Merkel's party may be at risk after squabbles and clashes since they are not aligned in their policies involving immigration of both parties. Though, Chancellor Merkel may be delaying the inevitable especially at a future time when her liberal administration is long gone and a new administration in power having to roll back all of her policies of welcoming migrants and providing a safe heaven for those who flee persecution. Recently, after faced with internal challenges and in order not to antagonize Germany's neighbours, Angela Merkel proposed a European Union wide solution to their crisis. She wanted to wait for an outcome of a summit of the Bloc's leaders on June 28, 2018. All this coming at the back of the election of the new Italian prime minister in June 2018 who refused to allow the ship Aquarius to dock at her port after carrying a load of rescued migrants from the Mediterranean Sea. However, Chancellor Merkel has warned that Seehofer's plan could shift the migrant burden onto countries such as Greece, Spain and Italy, where she is already unpopular for her economic and migrant policies. Recently, there's been no greater issue than the refugees and migrants' issue that has threatened to tear the Euro zone apart with Great Britain soon to finalize their deal to secede from this all-important Union, and who knows what country next, that might be voting to leave the Union. Leaders and incoming head of states have to face their citizenry and the political machinery of their countries to contest to power at the back of the hottest issue driving the greater momentum while dividing its people.

However, lawmakers from the Bavarian party (CSU) have backed Seehofer so far, giving him the nerve to defy his boss by going ahead with his plan without her agreement. Merkel is trapped between a rock and a hard place, a famous German Odysseus phrase. By their actions of fear and hostility, she could either rethink her own policy, correcting herself in everything she had done so far, being wrong. But she can't do that as she would be seen as a lame duck in her position as the Chief Executive of that country. She had alternative to either fire that minister. But then, her sister party would leave her coalition, which would leave her without a majority in parliament. That would be tough. In effect, that might mean going for another elections. It is unclear, if Angela Merkel would be voted into power again, although not impossible, should the German voters be sent back to the ballot box.

The Bavarian (CSU) party hardline stance might be argued that it came ahead of regional elections in Germany in October 2018, but the Bavarians have been seen in this light to fight against policies that are lenient over migrants as they also enact legislations that are unfriendly to migrants and asylum seekers extending to every part of their political system even the other arms of government are not spared, as they jointly support this system rejecting as many asylum seekers as possible denying them resident status in their beautiful country while demanding for a timeline and tougher approach towards deportations of failed asylum seekers. The government of Bavaria at the Southern border laments the migrant crisis at their border seeing it as a crucial issue even as they fear anti immigrant sentiments set in motion by their unnecessary anxiety and bitter politics could bring them down or end the party's dominance due to their harsh immigrant policy.

Many have criticized this party for putting its interests ahead of national unity as the politicians are the gainers of this policy as it brings them to power while spreading its divisive influence on its populace who are already reeling from the overwhelming impact of the national politics and foreign affairs driving racism tensions overboard. However, if you ask an ordinary German on the street on his take on immigration, as far as this administration's policies or the coming of migrants and asylum seekers into their country don't affect their jobs or social life, they don't have issues with it. The Bavarian party-CSU is risking a lot including the stability of the national government they are part of. Some already accused Seehofer of behaving like a Trump. They are making something out of nothing, and therefore with such sentiments they are allowing their panic to take Germany and Europe hostage. Some have alleged that Seehofer Christian Social Union wanted to change the law that automatically guarantees asylum to people facing persecution overseas especially Syria, replacing it with the power to accept or reject asylum seekers straight at the border. After a meeting of Horst Seehofer alongside Austria and Italy in July 5th, 2018, they agreed to introduce border controls. They even discussed closing off the entire southern route completely. Their decision brings the European Union's Schengen free travel zone into question with a number of the bloc's most influential countries looking to introduce border controls. The question is, why is the Christian Social Union taking a protective shade and alluring image under an umbrella of a moderate and progressive Christian Democratic Union of Angela Merkel led government while they are a typical example of a far-right wing movement promoting racial nationalism. Mrs. Merkel have had several crises talks with her opposition figure Mr. Seehofer within her government council, who also heads the Grand coalition's junior partner, the Christian Social Union. Maybe, this party with the far-right views know they will win ultimately as they grow into a position of recognition and dominance in an atmosphere of a complex agitation for change of asylum system not just in Germany but also in other European states including Italy. Since 2015 although, there is a scale back at the number of migrants coming into Europe to seek asylum, tensions between the European Union on how to handle this issue of irregular migration is dividing several member countries. Records show numbers are sharply down due to deal reached between the European Union and Turkey, New border fences in the Balkans, and a Bi-lateral arrangement between Italy and Libya. But the underlying cause that led to a surge in people coming to Europe since 2015 is not gone away. People believe as a result of this situation that is not addressed from the source nations, the tide of migration might peak again. However, statistics in recent times show that migration to the European Union has declined up to 90 percent since its peak in 2015. They keep using this date as a point of reference to the period, migration in Europe went to an all time high due to the conflicts in the middle east, but they also failed to state that migrants and refugees have been coming to Europe long before then, and Germany has shouldered much of that burden.

The policy makers are proposing that Europe change its asylum and immigration rules urgently. At present Italy and Greece bear more of the strain because of their geographical location, and the current rules states that asylum seekers must seek asylum at their first port of entry. That law does not do justice to the countries bearing the brunt of the influx, so they call it, and have been agitating for it to change for some time. But some seek for a tougher external border controls, others, a fair distribution of new arrivals. Solution will have to balance the concern of those at the southern frontiers while pushing back at hardliners such as Poland and Hungary even Bulgaria who are bent on not accepting migrants at all. With the anti immigration sentiments on the rise, the far-right party of Matteo Salvini and Italian Prime Minister Giuseppe Conte, which have campaigned and entered into power on the back of being hardline on migrants recently proposed deporting five hundred thousand people who are migrants in his country of Italy.

Though not literary supported by the majority of people in his country but the voices that backed him got stronger during the period of Italian elections and are still rearing their heads. The Italian economy is not healthy not for some time now as Italians themselves are seen moving out of their country in large numbers for better economic prospects in areas of education and seeking for jobs elsewhere. It's logical to say that the same reason that caused those Italian citizens to flee their country to Germany in search of greener pastures is the same reason that is driving those from Africa and Middle East. It's one world and we share one problem.

But the economic problems are at the summit of all the problems besieging whether it's eastern Europe, the Balkans, Greece or Italy or Africans who are risking their lives traveling and navigating through the dangers of Sahara arriving Libya. When they reach that North African country, they are locked up in holding centres, and those that were not found neither arrived Libya were killed on the way. They're reports of many being used as guinea pigs, as their organs are harvested for sale, some raped repeatedly, others forced into involuntary labour and if they refuse to labour against their will, they could face death. For those who finally succeed to get into boats to flee Libya, their journey to Europe could end before they arrive as they are given lousy boats that could break down at any time and risk drowning the lives of all those it carries just as it has happened over the years and it's still happening. European summits on migration crisis should not always be about the bickering of European member states over how too many migrants are coming in, or their distribution methods or their religion or lifestyles but about addressing the fundamental issues behind the migration of these people. Whether it's the problems of political instability, crisis, corruption, organized crime and poor economic state of the Africans and middle easterners who suffer the pain and trials on the road as they journey to Europe to seek for a good life, they should always seek to protect and save lives. They should remember, few can endure wars and crisis but even fewer can endure extreme poverty.

Therefore, emergency summit on economic investments are necessary, working with countries to improve their educational, economic opportunities and social security issues by ensuring education and healthcare is for all in every country where those migrants are coming from as well as addressing political issues of instability. Additionally, helping the governments to map out a framework to apply changes where necessary including setting up vital institutions that will help citizens to be vocationally trained, and after graduation those who need financial support are given to enable them to start their businesses as well as other social, economic and political structures to support growth. Vocational training has been seen and known to pay off in the end as an economic booster, just as Germany has done for its people and can testify on that area. People who can't go to universities or don't hope of ever finding better jobs because they are just not talented enough to attain a higher education are given opportunities to be trained on any aspect or profession of life whether be it as a carpenter, mechanic, technician, farmer, in manufacturing, computing, film making or in technology.

This situation can ensure jobs creation using the skills they derived from this policy which in turn sustains the economic society. This policy, if implemented, targeting millions of mostly the youth population, in the countries where migrants come from in association with the World bank, IMF and the governments of those countries would yield dividends that could arrest this situation in not more than ten years, if political will is applied to make sure it works. Graduands from the vocational training profession which last anywhere from three months to three years depending on what they study, are financially aided with loans or grants to enable them start up businesses of their choice while the government will set up a national committee with branches across the country to ensure the money given out to them does not go to waste as these recipients are attached with financial and creative market advisers and a market organized to ensure once their standard products are made, such as agricultural or manufacturing products, these well made products finds a market whether it's in China, America and Europe. In this manner, in the next five to ten years, reasons other than war prompting migrants and refugees to travel from their countries of birth in North and West Africa or Middle east could be arrested, to a greater extent. Moreover, the world will be better of, for it. Additionally, it will help to diversify the trading partners of Europe from mostly America, a situation which today they are held hostage to. Imagine, one powerful country like the United States of America with an autocrat as its head saying to other countries, you're nothing without us or you are under us because you need us more than we need you and we can do what ever we want with you". A case in point is the recent chaotic and dystopian unilateral trade policies of America targeting allies, damaging long-term relations and upsetting the peace and economic growth of the world.

That is the situation between America's Orwellian Trump and the world right now. Even, the American constitution made clear that no one person or organization should be allowed to be stronger or bigger than the country or put simply, 'above the law of that country and its regulations.' Then, why should the world watch in bitterness as America under Trump with his empirical policies are economically colonizing the world to their advantage alone. Unilaterally, undermining world institutions such as world trade organization and imposing tariffs on anything from grains to technological products to punish others who don't comply, sometimes for things unrelated while denigrating the idea of free trade. Such as in 2018 punishing Turkey for imprisoning an American Pastor, a situation if not controlled could plunge the Middle East and Europe into further political chaos as the Lira's further fall causing inflation and scarce resources could cause another major mass migration, if not controlled. Don't forget, Turkey hosts millions of refugees in their country, many of whom are working and earning a living from that country. Therefore, unintended or uncalculated consequences might bring Europe to a breaking point when the routes are flung open for migrants and refugees to move up in search for a better life. Come to think of it, is it not said, what's good for the goose is good for the ganda? America has in its prison cells tens of thousands of other countries citizens some bearing dual citizenship. "What if those countries demand for the release of their citizens?" Would their arbitrary and stringent Justice System that still relishes on exacting capital punishment while punishing minorities heavily for minor crimes, be compelled to release such foreign citizens who're accused of serious crimes?

On the other hand, America risk global peace and growth, punishing China with heavy tariffs, a country that has single-handedly transformed the state of the world's economy for the better since the beginning of the 21st century, a situation that might impact their larger population negatively even as it's perceived to be a trade war between the world powers for issues such as intellectual property thefts or other reasons, just to prove to China, America is still number one. "Tell me how they relate?" "Or, is it not the same issues of intellectual property rights that America skews to their advantage that have kept most of the world especially Africa in an underdeveloped state up until this day?" Not sharing innovative ideas and technology transfer has held Africa and many other countries in the world bogged down, and unable to leap to the next level. The worst aspect is that the United Nations Organization don't have a say because either they're complicit or are alienated in such important issues of peace and development because America has singlehandedly weakened its powers and ability for such an apex governing body to be actively in control of decision making over global issues and relying on it to proffer a collective solution to world problems. For how long will the world sit, wait and watch while the world disintegrates or further plunged into the abyss of horror, unnecessary tensions and economic destruction causing instability and mass migration by the activities of one authoritarian leader? At what time will the rest of the world including Germany rise and say enough is enough, while collectively putting in place the necessary instruments as a buffer to shield the world from such senseless economic and political turmoil as a result of unwarranted sanctions from an egomaniac?

It's like Britain, European Union and others sanctioning Zimbabweans for two decades and plunging this once thriving country into ruin, for the actions of one person, their former confused President Robert Mugabe. Or the uncalculated action of France, Britain and America in toppling President Gaddafi in Libya, and consequently throwing the whole country into chaos and political instability while opening up the country for international terrorists' groups to fester and thrive. Not to mention, the America's excuse of bringing down Saddam Hussein in Iraq, with the pretense that the country possesses weapons of mass destruction, and since 2003, the country has never remained the same as its terrorist enabled environment influence helps in destabilizing other nations, far and near. Once again, if he punishes Europe by raising taxes on things such as Auto and other products claiming the rest of the world have cheated America as they have trade imbalance, but still America is by far the wealthiest nation on the planet and will be like that for many years to come unless unforeseen circumstances occur such as financial crisis. And though, China is projected to take over that country in terms of Gross Domestic Products, America is fore-casted to remain the most attractive innovative market and world's super power nation on earth for several decades to come. But America, can't always gain around the world while fearing free trade and healthy competition, if not it will make them an uncontrollable economic monster, which might likely abuse their power beyond the era of Trump.

Going back to the issue of mass migration that has threatened the unity of the European Union bloc. As they try to regulate policies on how migrants are distributed when they enter Europe and tightening border control. The question now is, "how do migrants and refugees fleeing hunger, persecution and violence enter or get into Europe?" International migration for Organization estimates that more than one million migrants arrived by sea in 2015 and about 34,900 people by land. This compares with 280,000 arrivals by land and sea for the whole of 2014. The figures don't include those who got in undetected. If there's anything such as that, since one has to cross several borders to get to countries in the Southern, Northern and Western fronts. The European Union border force, Frontex, monitors the different sea routes migrants use and numbers arriving at Europe's borders and puts the figure that crossed into European territory 2015 at about 1,800,000. Most of those who came to Greece from Turkey took short voyage from Turkey to Islands of Kos, Chios, Lesvos and Samos, often in flimsy rubber or small wooden boats. The dangers associated with such journey can't be overemphasized. According to International Organization for Migration, more than 3,770 migrants were reported to have died or drowned trying to cross the Mediterranean in 2015. Most died from crossing from Libya to Italy, being the plied route for migrants from Africa to Europe. More than 800 died in the Aegean crossing from Turkey to Greece including the famous picture of a child named Alan Kurdi, whose tragedy on washing up on the beach sparked an International reaction or outrage. "Or, have the world forgotten that heart breaking image so soon?"

The summer months are mostly the busiest months for migrants attempting to reach Europe as fatalities occur during that time period. But in 2015, the deadliest month for migrants was April of that year, which saw a boat carrying about 800 people capsize in the sea of Libya. Overcrowding is thought to have been the primary cause of the disaster. On the other hand, which countries are most affected by this crisis? Although Germany has had the most asylum applications in 2015, Hungary had the highest in proportion to its population. Despite having closed its borders with Croatia in an attempt to stop the flow in October of that year. Nearly 1,800 refugees per 100,000 of Hungary's local population claimed asylum in 2015. But the country has since shut its borders to stem the flow of migrants into his country and Europe. Sweden followed behind with 1,667 per 100,000 of its country's population. The figure for Germany is 587 and for the U.K., it was 60 applications for every 100,000 residents. The European average was 260. In September of that year, European Union ministers voted by a majority to relocate 160,000 refugees European Union wide. The plan was to apply to those in Italy and in Greece as they bear the brunt of the migration inflow.

The failure of that policy has in part been responsible to many young teenagers in Greece and Italy who are now involved in prostitution rings as victims of this shadow evil lurking all over Europe including child gay prostitution as they feel left out in limbo, sometimes to make ends meet. Another 54,000 were to be moved from Hungary. Though, the government rejected the plan and would rather receive migrants from Italy and Greece instead as part of the relocation scheme. The United Kingdom among others opted out of the quota system. But according to the Home office figures 1000 Syrian refugees were resettled under the vulnerable persons relocations scheme in 2015. Even David Cameron, British prime minister said the United Kingdom will accept up to 20,000 refugees from Syria over the next five years. A promise they have held up to. But it's nowhere near that of their neighbouring counterparts.

Although huge numbers apply for asylum, the number of people given asylum is far lower. In 2015, European Union offered asylum to 292,540 refugees mostly from Syria due to the war in that country. In the same year more than a million applied for Asylum in Europe. Although these figures are often exaggerated, as Germany alone claims it took in a million migrants that year. So, whose estimates are false here? "Or, are they including the European Union or Eastern European migrants arriving in that country?" Refugee and Asylum application is a lengthy process, the number of people given asylum in that year in Germany may be from previous years.

On the 29th June 2018, the leaders of the European Union member countries met in Brussels in a storm of ever growing perceived crisis of migration in a bid to proffer solution or at least put a lid on the ever fuming and sparkling wine bottle after Italy and several other border European nations heads of state had threatened to stop migrants being dumped in their countries as first port of entry without other countries in the Union sharing in the burden of taking in migrants who are rescued from the high seas. At the end of the meeting concluded with decisions made on how to manage the issue, apart from some of the leaders of Nations in the Union caught up in this crisis, being positive about the way forward, allies of Angela Merkel has hailed talks in Brussels as toughening of the stance on Europe migration, but it's unclear if the deal would win over the Chancellor's staunchest critics and opponents in Bavaria and thus save her fraying coalition government, which at the time was making waves. Emerging from the summit on Friday morning, Angela Merkel said the joint message was a 'good signal.' While a lot of work was needed to create a joint Asylum system, the Chancellor, added. "I am confident that after today we can continue to work on this."

Gunther Oettinger, the European commissioner for Budget and Human resources described the outcome of the summit as a "Genuine Breakthrough." There are good reasons why the CSU-Christian Social Union will see this as a big step in the right direction. Oettinger told the German radio, "We in the CDU will recognize it as a big step in the right direction." The former Social Democrat leader Martin Schulz said the agreement was a pragmatic decision that should appease his interior minister, Horst Seehofer, who has threatened to start turning away migrants registered in the other European Union states from German borders, if Angela Merkel doesn't come up with a European solution by the end of July 2018. "Chancellor Merkel has given Horst what he wanted" Schulz told the WELT, adding that the statement's language of taking all necessary internal legislative and administrative measures to prevent secondary migration across the bloc's internal borders looked tailor-made for Seehofer's concerns. Martin Schulz, a former president of the European Parliament, predicted that a "coalition of the willing", consisting of Germany, France and Spain, would set up bigger processing centres for Asylum seekers inside the European Union, and called for more money from the European Union budget for those who volunteered to take an active role. The Bavarian Christian Social Union, which had created the pressure for Angela Merkel to emerge from the summit with a new deal on migration, had already deescalated before the German delegation went to Brussels. On the other hand, the German CSU delegate Hans Michelbach described the deal as a positive signal but does not rule out that his party's interior minister could decide to take drastic actions on the German border. "You have to recognize the path of a joint European Asylum policy is the right path,' he told the German ARD on Friday morning.

The question is, what it means for the national border and taking in of more migrants at the moment and in the coming months, is it necessary to take action immediately?" Since then, Angela Merkel meeting with her Bavarian party Christian Social Union in July 2018, to calm their concerns, have placed the direction of things at a different road and tempo as they had agreed to send back refugees registered in other European countries. Something the Bavarian allies of Merkel wanted and she without a choice heeding to their politics fearing the worst, if an agreement wasn't reached between the two sister parties and she having to fire her maverick Minister of Interior

Seehofer from his position. A situation that might result to their sister party pulling away from her coalition, and she left to go into another elections under a politically tense environment she's not sure to win.

Altogether, the fragile deal reached during the European Union summit was hailed as a success by the Italian populist Prime Minister Giuseppe Conte, who said it showed his country was no longer alone in dealing with the migrant crisis. But the Italian interior minister Matteo Salvini said in a morning talk show that progress has been made in principle on the issues of protecting the EU's external border and real investment in Africa. His tone however suggested a wait and see approach and reiterated that Italy would be closed to all NGO's involved in rescuing migrants from the sea. "They would only see Italy in a postcard." he added.

Far from endorsing any of the vague proposals that have been adopted, Salvini emphasized that Italy had an outsized role in the summit, and had succeeded in setting the agenda, forcing European Union partners to recognize its country's issues and problems.

Concerning the resolutions of the summit, secure centres for migrants may be set up in European Union states to process Asylum claims under a deal reached after the marathon summit. The controlled centres would be set up by the E.U. states on a voluntary basis and migrants whose claims were rejected would be sent back." Refugees could be settled in the EU states which agreed to take them. The deal follows weeks of diplomatic wrangling over migrant rescue ships and which country should take them in. Coastguard officials said on Friday, 29th June 2018, that around a hundred people were thought to have drowned off the Libyan Coast, with 14 rescued. They were found in waters to the east of the capital, Tripoli. The question is, where would the centres be built? There were no details on which countries might set up the secure centres or take in refugees, but the French President said, they will be in countries where migrants first arrived in the European Union. "We have struck the right balance between responsibility and solidarity," He said.

Numbers of migrants and asylum seekers entering the European Union have dropped over 90 percent since their 2015 peak, the European council says. Italy, the entry point for thousands of migrants, mainly from Africa threatened to veto the summit entire agenda, if it did not receive help. After this European Summit Europe is more responsible and offers more solidarity, said the Italian Prime Minister. Today, Italy is no longer alone." Other leaders struck a more cautious note. Angela Merkel said more needed to be done to resolve disagreements. European Council President said, "Too early to talk about success." We have managed to talk and reach an agreement. But this is in fact the easiest part of the process, compared to what awaits us on the ground when we start its implementation, he told a News Conference. During the meeting it was agreed also that jump off centres would also be established in North Africa. This is another ambitious partnership with Africa. That's the European Union trying to balance its tough migrant entry approach on the inside with a friendly external one and offering incentives to North African countries to host facilities where migrants can be assessed for resettlement in Europe. The European Union also agreed other measures including: Strengthening external borders and boosting finance for Turkey and countries in North Africa.

Secondly, exploring the possibility of regional disembarkation platforms, aimed at breaking the business model of people smuggling gangs by processing refugees and migrants outside the European Union. However, getting North African countries to agree on such resolutions could be difficult and Morocco already rejected the idea.

Thirdly, internal measures taken by the member states to stop migrants from moving within the European Union, which the agreement said undermined asylum policy and the border free Schengen travel area.

Fourthly, more investments in Africa to help the continent achieve a substantial socioeconomic transformation. So that people no longer leave for a better life.

Fifth, further work to reform European Union asylum policy, including changes to the Dublin regulation under which migrants must be considered for asylum in the first safe country where they arrive. About 56,000 asylum seekers have arrived Europe this year from January to end of June in 2018, said the International Organization for Migration. That's a fraction compared to a million people that arrived in Europe in 2015. The question is, if the plan is still vague or not implemented as planned and European states such as Italy and Malta start turning away migrants at their borders brought in by NGO's, who then would be responsible for these migrants at sea. In furtherance of what happened when Italy and Malta refused to accept migrants rescued by the Aquarius ship, the charitable rescuers. What about those treated as slaves in the Libyan detention centres operated by the government. The Lifeline boat was only allowed to dock in Malta after intense diplomacy among several European Union states, who each agreed to take a part of the migrants rescued. Malta said Norway, had agreed as well to take in a share of the migrants. Medecins Sans Frontieres-MSF had branded the new European Union deal as inhumane. The only thing they have appeared to have agreed on is to block people at the doorstep of Europe, regardless of how vulnerable they are or what horrors they are escaping and to demonize non-governmental search and rescue operations, added MSF emergencies chief Karline Kleijer.

Throughout history, people had migrated from place to place, call it whatever you want, whether as tourists, business travelers, immigrants, students for studies abroad, or migrants and refugees fleeing conflicts and persecutions. If possible for migrants, they would seek legal ways of reaching Europe, but such ways are difficult and take time. Time is what they don't have because some of these people flee persecutions, violence, wars, extreme poverty and excruciating pain. More also young people try reaching abroad such as Europe because they want to reunite with their families, benefit from a good educational system, and to stop their unborn children from experiencing the horrors they themselves faced. Since 2015 and 2016, Europe experienced an unprecedented number of migrations into its borders, most of them especially from Syria fleeing war and terror as well as other countries in Africa in a deep hole in between the war of terrorist's organizations fighting the governments of their countries. Though, the European Union has agreed on a range of resolutions of dealing with the situation, including setting strategies in place to make peace in places where war currently exists as well as increasing humanitarian aid to people in desperate need of them both inside and outside the European Union. Also distribute asylum seekers evenly among the union, resettle people in need in Europe and return those who don't qualify for asylum.

The question today is that those measures of granting asylum to seekers who truly need it are not met as the day progresses various nations and states even regions within countries are setting new standards for granting asylum to persons fleeing danger and violence. In some cases, no matter what you say, it's straight out rejected by the immigration department. The courts which are supposed to be impartial are dragged into this situation as many court rooms are partisan now. They follow the politics of the day, and as humans, they have their biases as well. A case in point, in Germany, the situation was better a few years ago, before 2015 as the judicial system looks critically into a situation and serves justice where due. But now especially those in the Bavarian area caught up in this migration sentiments and inhumane reactions it gets from its majority party, it refuses many especially from Africa, and Middle east, regardless of the evidence they have, also considering other prejudices set as Asylum regulations by the National legislative parliament. Thereby echoing the sentiments held by the government and CSU in Bavaria and other bigots in the opposition parties such as the Alternative for Deutschland (AfD).

It was bad before now getting asylum in this region of Germany but in recent times, it's gone worse. And the same people, will be shouting on top their voices of how many refugees and migrants they have provided with sanctuary. What is the good of a sanctuary when it's not a permanent one and you're sending the person after a while to go right back to the place he or she dreaded and fled to seek a better and safe life in Europe. "If that's not comedy tell me what it is?"

The judiciary in a way might be afraid of granting asylum to individuals especially from the countries and regions considered safe or countries in West Africa, they are not compatible with, and if granting sanctuary to the suffering migrants who fled to that country, would make them liable to be investigated, that situation makes them tougher in cases that were supposed to be a free pass based on testimony and evidence. So, there's corruption and no sector is left out in this political onslaught, as none of them are strong enough to independently do what they think is right, fearing backlash from other parties especially if they are generous enough. But no one is talking about generosity but those who merit it are in recent times no longer qualified for the system asylum. That tantamount to bigotry at the highest level. Everyone is careful on this sensitive issue and don't want to be caught up in the web of the accusations often associated with doing the right thing these days.

Just like it happened in the North of Germany in Bremen early in April and May 2018, when the migration department there were accused of being generous with their residence status by granting several thousands of people a legal stay in the country claiming some were given without following the due process. You see headlines in the national News gazettes such as 4,500 asylum cases to be re-examined after Bremen's migration office scandal. Following a scandal at the immigration office in Bremen branch, thousands of asylum cases are liable to be reviewed to know if they were well deserving to be granted asylum and to toughen policies in place. It said, a former director at the immigration department known as BAMF, branch office granted at least 1,200 people asylums claiming the proper conditions were not met. Federal investigators were sent to investigate the case who was said to have granted asylum to migrants between 2013 to 2016 with a team of lawyers. In most cases the applicants were said to be Yazidis, a kurdish religious minority. In response, the federal ministry of Interior led by the same political detractor Seehofer promised a thorough investigation of the asylum seekers who benefited from the scam, so they said. "So, it's all a farce?" Are these authorities' intentions not genuine after all? Trying to impress the world when in actuality they are not doing enough internally to resettle migrants.

Laws keep on changing as the migration issue evolves. No humanity face is given to those who deserve to be pitied. "What's wrong with granting Asylum to the Yazidis?" "Are these not the same people whom we learned, were raped, tortured, persecuted, extremely violated, their houses burnt, communities destroyed and almost 10,000 people killed or kidnapped by Islamic State or ISIS?" If it were possible to some nations, political parties or populist individuals within the Euro zone to deport everyone in their countries other than their white citizens just to make a political stance, send a message or for some gain, they would do so. Just like the New Italian far right government said they will deport hundreds of thousands of people back to their countries due to anti immigrant sentiments allowed to fester and simmer into the fabric of that country. It's the same situation that happens in Germany that takes place in Italy as one woman once puts it, "I have never seen a country so racist like Italy." The people detest the sight of migrants on their streets. Tell me, how could those people ever give a stay and path to citizenship to an asylum seeker when they don't regard such as a human being who's on the same level as they are.

CHAPTER FIVE

THE AMERICAN MIGRANT AND FOREIGN POLICY

In America, from the very inception of the Orwellian and autocratic Donald Trump administration, Immigration has been a defining issue as his rhetoric during the American election primaries echoed these sentiments calling for a tougher or zero tolerance approach and penalties towards migrants and refugees fleeing poverty, war and persecution who come in crossing through the US-México border. But the spring time and summer 2018 surge in migrant children who have been separated from their families after crossing America's southern border spurred a migrant crisis. The rhetoric got heated as detractors and opposition member parties invoking some of history's gravest human rights abuses as they accuse the nation's administrations of unconscionable cruelty.

In April 2018, the United States attorney General Jeff Sessions announced that the administration would begin pursuing a zero-tolerance policy towards adults who illegally cross the border. "If you're smuggling a child, we'll prosecute you and that child would be taken away from you as required by law", He said. "If you don't like that, then don't smuggle children through our border." A 1997 court settlement, legal precedent dictates that children must be detained in the least restrictive setting possible while cases are processed. A subsequent ruling found that the rule applies to both unaccompanied minors. Those who cross alone and those who cross with their parents. Under those guidelines, children who cross the border fall under the custody of the department of health and human services. The Trump administration mandating prosecutions as a result of the zero-toleance policy puts parents into criminal proceedings as they're locked up in high security prisons while splitting their families. A situation that saw migrant parents and others put in chains, and arrested, put into holes, and a tracker device to monitor their movement placed on them. "I don't want kids taken away from their parents, but when you prosecute parents for coming in illegally, which should happen, you have to take the children away", Mr. Trump said during a speech regarding the heated issue. Federal data showed that more than 2,000 children were separated from their families at the border over a six-week period spanning mid-April and May and from early may to June 2018.

As the criticism mounts spurred on by the images and audio of kids placed into shelters away from their parents, the Trump administration vigorously pushed back on the motion they are not to blame. The American president repeatedly blamed democrats, their opposition party, claiming falsely, that a law they championed is at fault. Even his homeland secretary said, 'We do not have a policy of separating families at the border, period." Deflecting blame during a combative white house press conference. "Congress created this mess and congress alone can fix it", She said. The entire time, critics and human rights activists are blasting Trump administration's policies as inhumane, cruel and as government approved human rights abuse. A situation of heat that prompted the country to quit the United Nations Human Rights council, rather blaming the council for having human rights abusers on the table whose country has done worst things in comparison to her country that champions human rights law within the country and abroad.

Of course, there was no way they could defend such inhumanity and cruel way they treat migrants who flee terrible things to seek asylum and a good life in America. And although, it's true the country has championed that cause for a long time, but from the very moment they relented in helping those in need rather forcing them to return to the same situation that forced them to come to America or prosecuting such people, from that time, which of course effectively started during the tenure of Trump, they seized to be accorded such respect and title they deserved as leaders or human rights champions.

"Tell me, if a country as the United States quits such a body of World human rights decision making body, regarding their administration's zero tolerance policy on fellow human beings who seek their help, what right do that country have to preach to any nation with regards to human rights violations or abuses in those countries?" Don't forget those countries are many in the world. It's a sad situation that the period of administration of Trump only brings pain, sorrows and wars to ordinary poor people of not just his country but around the world. Or, the recent situation where he announced the removing of the United States embassy from the present capital to Jerusalem. Against all cry of resistance amongst world leaders and other organizations even the common people of that land, defying the peril of the common residents of Palestine, he did it any way because he doesn't care what others think, and that only what he thinks or America's position, which of course was supported by many in the Republican party, would happen. If that's not the actions of an unstable and troublesome ruler, then what it is? "What is the difference between this man and the North Korean leader, whom his country's media stations call a dictator?" Although, he desisted from using such word, but equally the same, for a country like America whose institutions are solidly laid on the ideals of humanity, liberal democracy and freedom, to have a president who defies the people and congress and even those in his cabinets to do whatever he wants is simply sad, and therefore, the country's role and significance in the wider world should be reassessed. Many people died as a result of such decision to relocate the American embassy to Jerusalem as protesters of such policy were met with bombs, fire and fury by the Israeli military, who without compassion continue to subject the poor people of Gaza in Palestine in perpetual slavery without rights nor freedom to the outside world. The same support they got from America made the Israeli legislature to make recent binding and narcissistic laws such as declaring the country exclusively as the nation state of the Jewish people while discriminating against the Arabs and reducing the Arabic from being an official language to a language of special status.

As all this is happening in 2018 and might continue into the foreseeable future, the question some people keep on asking is, what are the world leaders saying concerning this, regarding the new autocratic principles and behavior of the United States and Israel. Humanity to Humanity seems dead under this time period of the coming to power of Donald Trump. The same person decimated the authorities of world bodies such as the United Nations and other important world organizations, as he attacks and reducing them to almost nothing with his ways, words and conducts such as the Paris global warming summit treaty and the United States commitment and compliance to ensure they cut green house gases to zero as the world is getting heated through the industrial activities of humans in various countries on earth, especially that of America and China. He has put back the USA-CUBA sanctions, the very one his predecessor toiled to get lifted. He calls Mexican criminals, rapists and drug peddlers, while attacking their authorities for sending the worst people into his country. He doesn't like Germany because they sell their well-made manufactured products and are prosperous on the multiple backs of America. Moreover, he dislikes any country and their head of state in the West that takes in migrants into their country in Europe especially from the Islamic nations. He is standing against anything good and sane in the world. He doesn't like China because they are thriving to grow and even surpass America with partly the technology they share with or he claimed they stole from America, that very idea or future projection of China beating America, makes him crazy, and would want to see them brought down. Once again, if that's not the action of a vampire whose voraciousness of other's energy to sustain his is insatiable, then, tell me what is it?

Once again, what are the other world powers doing to stop or sanction him, to make sure he realizes the world is shared by all people and not just his proud powerful country? But, No, how could Europe or Asia level sanctions against an all-powerful United States of

America, when the same country controls a majority index of their gross domestic product and economic output or forecasting indicators and when they do that, they would be directly shooting themselves on the foot and head at the same time. Like the American media said, Europe needs America more than America needs Europe. But that pales in comparison to what he does to his own country men and women, as he incites xenophobia, narcissism, hatred, discrimination, sexism and bigotry, thereby empowering far right groups such as the group called the KuKluxKlan to continue to stoke their fires of hate and white supremacy. That situation has indeed caused several deaths in that country in recent times, where loners rise with guns to go into black churches to killing everyone or see signs placed in streets that have the racism handwriting all over it. Or, the police brutality towards defenseless black minority. Even normalizing it, making everyone to have such tendencies to attack the black man even the black policemen attacking their fellow blacks, because they operate under a system that has normalized that racial prejudice, as its brain washed them, using them as instruments of brutality against their fellow brethren. A situation that does little to dampen the memory and pain of the 400 year old transatlantic slavery that rocked that country as the white slave masters used a heavy and high handedness to mistreat, torture, punish, lynch, rape and violently took away the identity of their fellow black brothers and sisters, even as those who resisted were summarily killed, all in the name of superiority towards others. The very situation that caused the American civil war. The same people that used the Holy Bible to preach love, unity, freedom, liberty and despite the enthronement of democracy dictating the rule of law and the equality of all people under the law and before God even as stated in the declaration of Independence, they never stopped being brutish and violent towards their fellow black people as former slaves, and in spite of calls to end discrimination, bigotry, hate and brutality, they didn't until in the 1960's African American civil rights movement in America, after many sacrifices were made in the name of freedom for the black man.

A renaissance of that sad past is turning up, as most actions of America's Trump, outside using them for political gain, does little to stem the tides of the ugly brute that is once again rearing its ugly head and dividing not just his own but those in Europe as tolerance is thrown out into the dustbin. The world is at a junction, a crossroads point where if it doesn't turn back, it will incur a deep wound in the heart of the soul of our very modern civilization, whose hands could prove difficult again to be turned back. If the powerful and rich or mighty politicians in countries, such as in Africa, Middle East, Eastern Europe, South East Asia or South America continues to deride human freedom and punish opposition members, or those groups of people that are fighting for freedom or for equal rights, and the United States' actions, only echoes the same sentiments seen as legitimizing or supporting their actions, what moral ladder do they have to walk on, an example to look up to? Of course, they would use America's impudence or negligence to these basic rights or their trampling on them, to further their reign of impertinence and brutal crackdown of their enemies or opposition in their countries. It's simple.

Recently, after Donald Trump was declared the winner of the Presidential race in his country, he declared a total shutdown and ban of all Muslims entering into the United States, until the country's officials figure out what's going on." He echoed the same words he used during his campaign as presidential candidate claiming large segment of the Muslim population have hatred towards America. Days after a married Muslim couple carried out a deadly shooting attack on the American soil in San Bernardino, California, his team released a statement December 7, 2015 about the proposal of a total shutdown of all Muslims entering into America, until he figures out what was going on. Trump said polling and research backed his concerns over Muslims. But polling experts questions its validity and the centre that issued the poll warned against generalizations. In July 21, 2016: We must immediately suspend immigration from any nation that has been compromised by terrorism until such as time as proven vetting mechanisms have been put in place. He even signed two executive orders to temporary halt the entry of Muslim nationals from several Muslim majority countries in the Middle east and Africa. He said, the countries were selected due to their connection with terrorism. "To be clear, he said, this is not a Muslim ban as the Media falsely reports it. This is not about religion. This is about terror and keeping our country safe." In spite of the outcry and the actions of several states including Washington State to block the implementation of that Executive order and the massive rally and support from the public shown to Muslims as seen all over the nation's Airport, he continued to defy the people to do as he pleases.

Back to the crisis, instability and wars rocking some Middle eastern countries, these had been partially enabled by the world's powerful nations including the United States and the United Nations inadequacies and incapacity to meet the growing demands of the world and its ability to reassess its policies, constitution and why it was established in the first place. If the United Nations or the World's powerful nations find it difficult to monitor, guide, support both material and moral as well as set a standard example as the shinning light for the rest of the other nations to follow, then, the strength of their influence, role and significance in world affairs is diminished, and in such a situation they could be a breakdown in the basic principles of human freedom, the exact situation that characterizes the reality of political and social life in many nations on earth today. This is not a situation where the world points a finger at Africa and using words like corruption. The state of the world's fall is beyond just beyond corrupt, but human lives and freedom are at stake. The world has the past to learn from and the tools in our reach to make it work. In the Middle East today, there are wars such as in Yemen and Syria. There are also occupations such as the Palestinian authority being occupied by Israel with the full support and backing of America. If the powerful nations of the world created the brute and perp, whose world policies' overtime were of course responsible for most of the injustices and regimes of terror rocking the world today, they should once again be able to fight to put the mindless and uncontrollable fascist brute back into a leash where it belongs. But like every other thing in life it's easier to destroy than to build. The British created the State of Israel following the defeat of the Ottoman Empire in World War 1, as Britain assumed control of Palestine. In November 1917, the British government issued the Balfour Declaration, announcing its intension to facilitate the establishment in Palestine, a national home for the Jewish people due to the anti-anti-Semitism against these people.

Today, the British don't even have a say on what is going on there. The brutal treatment of Palestinians by the Israeli government and military. Americans on the other hand, that empowers it, financially, technologically and economically only inflames the situation. Are those the actions of a nation, a powerful one for that matter that claims to be the world's mediator and peacemaker?

When President Obama tried to do something about it during his tenure, he was attacked by the opposition elite calling him a Muslim or African other than American born, a searing blistering attack and prejudice sponsored by then businessman Donald Trump to de-legitimize Obama. Throughout his tenure, Obama's stance on the actions of Israel made him least popular among that nation's political elites and opposition members. When one watches the American presidential primaries and main elections, and how a potential candidate or one aspiring to become a President of that country, is being asked to vow to back Israel and to make a speech in a democratic forum that would make them seem they are not against the State of Israel, then I wonder, is that freedom that America professes? For example, during Trump's speech to the American Israel public affairs' committee, a powerful Pro-Israel lobbying group, was part of a day long effort by the anti-establishment candidate to throw his support for Israel, and so do Hillary Clinton. He described himself as extremely Pro-Israel saying Palestinians would have to be willing to accept that Israel will forever exist as a Jewish state and able to stop attacks on Israelis. "They must come to the table knowing that the bond between the United States and Israel is unbreakable," Trump stated. Israel has erred in several ways, which it wasn't criticized for. In recent years especially under the reign of Benjamin Netanyahu, who has used maximum force to treat the people of Palestine and Gaza in particular, in a sinister and horrific manner. Then, there's the racism against Israeli Arabs on the part of the Israeli State and some Israeli people identified by critics as ranging from personal attitudes, to their portrayal in the media, education, immigration rights, housing segregation and social life in general.

Finally, there's the horrific discrimination of black Africans and migrants in Israel. A government plan to deport 34,000 African migrants back to Rwanda or Uganda has provoked more hand wringing than usual. Come to think of it, Israel itself was created by refugees and survivors of the Holocaust. The government proposed a plan to offer financial incentives including payment of 3,500 dollars to African migrants who agree to leave Israel voluntarily and go to Rwanda or Uganda. It said that those who don't agree to leave may be expelled by force or imprisoned. Under which scriptures of any religion or tradition of any society is it taught that it's only force that can conquer the opposition, enemy or evil? Yes, Americans dropping a Nuclear Bomb in Hiroshima, Japan, and destroying that city and its people, with scars that are still evident today among the people as a reminder, a strategy that made them win the war, forcing Japan to surrender in world war 2, doesn't mean it will always work like that all the time.

Especially in today's world where conventional war tactics are no longer effective as the enemy has practically evolved. With such guerrilla warfare fought around the world in several nations from Middle East to Africa even used by terrorists explains why in today's world just going to war to bomb a nation, may not be enough. That situation might provide the exact opposite of what was intended as it would further split that country into little pieces headed by militias who will then unite to fight their enemy in a war that recent history has shown cannot be won with just extreme prejudiced force alone.

Once again, having seen how the world has changed since the American invasion of Afghanistan in 2001 and second invasion of Iraq in 2003, it should give the world especially the powerful nations cause to pause and rethink their tactics and strategy for going to war with any group of people or nations. This explains why no matter the bombs, Israel launches at Gaza or back and forth, will never resolve the situation. They know what they have done wrong, and I suggest, they should go to the drawing board to address things starting by freeing the people and land of Palestine. Secondly, show them love by helping them technologically with logistical support from America to transform their neighbouring country to resemble theirs, and with the help from their rich gulf nations like Qatar, irrespective of how small their land is, they might rise and fulfill their potentials and become rich with investments raining in from mostly other rich middle eastern nations. I think, if Israel show that country love and solidarity rather than fire for fire or an eye for an eye, then the situation will be redeemed. If not, they might be doomed to continually face those crises plaguing them for a long time to come.

On the other hand, we have, Yemen that since 2015 have endured violence, pain and outright destruction by Saudi Arabia and their allies who today don't have the moral right to even speak of the bad treatment meted against other smaller nations in the middle east like Palestine and Syria. They have ordered military equipment worth billions from America and Europe which they use in killing innocent men, women and children of that country. The United Nations recently warned in 2018 that up to a million people might die while many others would suffer from hunger and malnourishment, if that war is not stopped. But what do the world powerful nations do instead? They further their sale of weapons to Saudi Arabia and United Arab Emirates for money to grow their military hardware establishments to deploy in the further destruction of Yemen. Once again, this is another example of how force may never win a war. It is presently termed the "world worst forgotten war." There are disappearances, arbitrary detentions, killings, untold torture, hunger and other crimes against humanity happening in that war-torn country, being perpetrated by Saudi Arabia and its coalition.

Where is the role of the Media in all of this? Of course, it's an unpopular war, it might not give them the ratings they need to score more integrity and value for reward and growth from its American or western audience. So, the result is to not care by covering that war in contrast to what they did in Iraq or Syria. If the Media played their role effectively in this war, just maybe, the Americans or the world's super power nations might force Saudi Arabia to end the war. Once again like the Israel-Palestine situation and American invasion of Iraq, force is not the answer to an ever-evolving enemy who is determined to die for a cause. Others call it a proxy war for Iran and Saudi Arabia, as Iran fuels the war by keeping up the constant supply of money, people and equipment including missiles for the local militias to use to engage their enemy. Whether their source of defense is coming from Iran, and whether America or Israel blames Iran for the spread of missiles to Gaza or now Houthi in Yemen, and proposing sanctions against them for their involvement in the terror activities that is going on around the middle east or not, can't change the fact that, lives and freedom are at stake, and the approach they currently take, is not leading to anywhere neither is the imposition of sanctions and alienation of Iran, the best strategy.

So, how many in Yemen must die before America, Europe and the United Nations come together to resolve that conflict which by the way is not beyond them. They know exactly what to do, and the war on either side might no longer continue. But politics always take centre stage, as the rest of the world watch in despair when the images appear on their television stations, and only hope that the situation is resolved and peace reigns. Imagine, the number of migrants from Yemeni alone that have fled the slaughter, violence and deaths into other neighbouring countries, the burden it creates for the neighbouring countries especially the poorer ones around them. Because countries like Saudi Arabia and the UAE might be protective of their countries, screening the fleeing migrants and refugees they take in, not to incur the wrath of their enemy. That situation might make them not to be receptive towards the migrants fleeing war, violence and hunger, the way they are supposed to. The same war which United Arab Emirates helped to create as they joined their Saudi forces in Yemen to attack their Houthi forces, even as they fear a retaliation that might make them not to take in the many refugees from that war like the American President Trump would say, they're infesting our beautiful country. The United Arab Emirates was implicated in disappearances, detain and torture abuse of many people in Yemen suspected to be part of the war. Other migrants who flee to their beautiful country in search of jobs are exploited as migrant workers. Migrant construction workers face serious exploitation in that country without proper accommodation including other innocent young girls being trafficked for sexual slavery in the United Arab Emirates.

According the International Organization for Migration, Saudi Arabia has expelled over 17,000 migrants so far, from January 2018 to May 2018, amidst fears that it could deport almost 700,000 migrants more back to war and misery in their homeland, thereby deepening the crisis more in Yemen. Saudi Arabia has been imposing fines, jail-time and deportation of migrants caught without valid identity documents in a bid to reduce its black market in labour. They are returned back because of not possessing a valid documents or right immigration status in Saudi Arabia. This applied to irregular migrants being returned to countries such as Bangladesh, the Philippines and Ethiopia. How can the same country bombing Yemeni be returning people fleeing their bombs and gunfire? Why couldn't they waive this until Yemenis have a country to return back to.

It could be recalled that Saudi led coalition backed by the West have carried out airstrikes against the Houthi movement in a war since 2015 to restore the Internationally recognized government. The Iran aligned Houthis control about 70 percent of Yemen, including the Capital Sanaa. Ten thousand have been killed already in a war that has displaced over three million already internally and presently unleashed one of the world's worst humanitarian crisis in recent history. Apart from Yemenis fleeing the barrel of the gun and airstrikes are other migrants from Africa, many detained, subject to abuse and extortion by smugglers. Some 7,000 migrants arrive each month from mostly Ethiopia, Somalia and Eritrea who transit Yemen in hopes of reaching Saudi Arabia. International Organization for Migration said it helped about 2,700 people in 2017 to get back home. More inmates want to be returned home from Yemeni instead of living like animals in holding facilities in the war-torn country. Officials of the U.N. Agency said taking them back home is no problem but getting the permission for deconfliction to have the organization's buses travel from Sanaa to Hodeidah to advance security guarantees. The clearance they hoped to get in order to start the initial operation of moving migrants, the majority being Ethiopians.

In 2017, Britain and other European countries were accused of breaching International Law, as the number of asylum seekers forced to return to Afghanistan had tripled at a time at a time when civilian casualties were at a record high. Despite Afghanistan being declassified from post conflict to active conflict by the United Nations in 2017, asylum seekers acceptance rates for Afghans have declined sharply over the past two years, the NRC report found. The majority of people displaced within Afghanistan in 2017 were from Nangarhar Province, in the east, and from the North west Province of Kunduz. About 84 percent of people from Nangarhar said the area was now under ISIS control, while 97 percent from Kunduz reported that their homes were now under the jurisdiction of Taliban. The NRC found an increase in child labour and child marriage among the displaced. Only 25 percent of displaced families receiving aid. Afghans constitute one of the largest and longest displaced refugee groups in the world, with three million living in Pakistan and Iran. More than one million Afghans have been newly displaced by the conflict in the past two years-a threefold increase in less than five years. In 2017, an average of 1,200 Afghans were forced to flee each day, including Afghan refugees who were forced to return home, the report said. Remember, the United States along with allies invaded Afghanistan in late 2001, after the September 11th attacks in America. The conflict was known as the US war in Afghanistan. Its public aims were to dismantle Al Qaeda, and to deny it a safe base of operations in Afghanistan by removing the Taliban from power. Almost two decades on, the Afghan invasion was only an arrogant, wretched and doomed adventure that caused nothing but untold pain, agony, deaths and a huge migrant crisis while the problems still persist. The democracy is fledgling, corruption festers, poverty is pervasive, the social infrastructures are weak and most importantly the terror groups are not defeated. The question is, have the Americans and allies, after all these years achieved what they set out to accomplish?

Lastly, the war in Syria which has defied all remedies, if they were ever any, provided they stop the suffering of the innocent men, women and children, whose over ten million citizens have either fled or are internally displaced rendering the entire nation destroyed and only reduced to rubbles with no part of the country spared in the onslaught. It's painful to see President Assad continues to be in that seat of power or hold tight to that position being supported by Russia, another battle ground used as proxy war for the world's powerful nations. Like a friend, I know in Germany told me a nerve-racking story of himself and his family. Their story of survival could be termed unique but truly nothing is unique in these strange and violent times. Whatever one faced, another may have seen worse. He said, after the 2011 revolution, initially during the beginning period of the resistance, he was one of those arrested and imprisoned along with other protesters. He stayed in jail for over three years, and in-spite of the efforts of relatives to free him and others at the peak of the war in 2013 and 2014, it was futile. But eventually, they found someone who negotiated for their release with some monies paid. When he got out he realized that their house and many other homes in city of Homs were destroyed as many of their people had fled to the neighbouring countries including Jordan and Lebanon, and his cousin and sister, had all died in the war due to the sheer force of the Assad bombs that were raining down on that city by the country's military forces.

After he was released, his parents having lost everything including their livelihood, they decided to flee to either Jordan, Lebanon or should go to Turkey where they have a better chance to further their journey to Europe for a better life. He reached Turkey later part of 2014 and had to stay for the next months along with his remaining brethren and parents. Finally, in the middle of 2015, when the story of migrants fleeing to Greece came to their knowledge, having worked for a couple of months, he saved up some money, along with his parents they paid traffickers, who'll get them across the sea to the other side in Crete or Lesbos. His boat was ready earlier as he was called to join an inflatable boat, and although the boat was packed full in a dangerous journey that might see them perish, they entered anyway, and rode all night in a turbulent sea to evade the coast guards. They finally succeeded to steer the boat by themselves until reaching the border frontier of Greece in Lesbos Island. According to Abdullah, reaching there was a thing of joy as before their travel, they had heard stories of many people who had perished or lost their lives in the sea due to the turbulence of the sea.

The next step was to begin their 15-day journey to Munich through Serbia that might eventually lead them to Hungary. They were lucky that by that time the focus on the migrant's journey was not much publicized as those who journeyed through that route from Greece to Macedonia to Serbia made it to Hungary, a jump off point to the rest of the European Union. He was one of a group of migrants, as after days on the road reaching Hungary against all odds, he was now more than ever that they were close to their destination. Some from their group had made up their minds to go to Sweden, other Netherlands while more of them to Germany. He was one of those who chose Germany not because he had a relative in that country but because he has heard that the country's policies along with Sweden was generous to Syrians and was sure to have a better life, and probably education and a good job when he gets to Germany.

They then proceeded on that journey that took them evading authorities not to register their finger prints in those countries, as they headed to Austria with a train. Reaching Austria, they were interrogated by the authorities, but opted out of registering in Austria, as they finally boarded a train from Austria to Germany, the land of their dreams. Reaching there in Munich, they were shown the way, to the Migration office, as they went there to regularize their papers and were eventually taken care of, and he was sent to Wuezburg in Bavaria. I met him in German language school, as he narrated his story to me. What happened to your folks and parents?" I asked him. "They perished in the sea on their way crossing over to Greece," he told me. But my other brother and sister who were not on the same boat survived, He said to me. Where are they now" I asked. "On the road, In Greece but hopefully, they might succeed just as I did and join me here in no time," Abdullah added.

Later that year in 2015 and in 2016 would see hundreds of thousands of Syrians mostly cross the Mediterranean to Europe. While millions of others are scattered throughout the region seeking refuge in Lebanon, Turkey and Jordan as those who bore the brunt of the crisis in Syria making it the world's worst humanitarian crisis since world war two. Even, though Europe is squeaking and yelling at each other claiming this crisis of migration might tear their union apart, and the recent summit in Brussels in June 29th, 2018 having Theresa May, saying to the European leaders, to care for their own citizens first. It makes me wonder, "Britain again?" If that doesn't echo a familiar sentiment and phrase popularly used by Donald Trump and the 'Britain First' Fascist group, I wonder what does.

If the British where in the position of Germany, I think they might probably break or divide, I mean literally, considering the way the same issue made the former Prime Minister David Cameroon to resign from his position. He promised if the people voted No, in a referendum, he held in 2016, he'll quit. But it's not just the immigration that was the British problem as the country always thought of itself better than the rest of the other Union members, as if the world was still in the 19th century or early twentieth century when, the British thought they were the super nation on earth, winning every war, and establishing their influence and imprints on almost every country or continent on earth. Like what one German senior citizen, Mr. Werner,

I saw in the old people's care home where I did vocational study practicals, told me. He said that after the second world war he traveled to Britain to live and study. And In that time, Britain would organize international football tournaments. It was termed "Britain and the rest of the world." What arrogance? He added with laughter. "Really?" I responded. "Was there no FIFA at the time?" He laughed. "Yes, there was," he told me. But remember this was immediately after the war. "We were the gentle giants who instead of suppressing our protectorates and colonies, would rather show them the light with a gentle touch," they said

That makes me think the main reason for their separation from the European Union was to send a message, a familiar one, they'd always sent. Why would a country agree to and operate under a common Union but don't follow the rules of that Union? That's Britain, still maintaining the British Pounds and closing their borders to foreigners in the Schengen Union or in the least, restricting the freedom of movement, social welfare and integration of the citizens of the same Union they belong to especially those in Eastern Europe, the very cornerstone ideals that defines the creation and existence of such Bloc. Even if in my opinion Germany was more solid, economically stronger and aesthetically appealing than England or the United Kingdom but allowed visitors and tourists in the union to come into their country with their Schengen Visas. What then does that say about the United Kingdom and their strengths of inclusion or attitude of exclusion towards others?

They have always wanted to quit. The land of the Queen Elizabeth II, and most influential monarchy in the whole world, when in my opinion the Queen does not support the Brexit move, she never did. Because on the day of the referendum for Brexit in the United Kingdom, she wore a dress brilliantly radiating the stars of the European Union, and without saying a word, she emphasized her position using what she wore, the various colours and map of the Union. It's not hard for the British people and their leaders to figure that out. They knew exactly where their Queen stood. But the monarchy has an extent of influence and under a democratic political administration, it wouldn't want to interfere or force anyone to follow their footstep in order not to be criticized. The last thing they want is an uproar caused by the Queen, a situation she caused with her own hands whose effects might come to bite the British people, and the people later blaming her for influencing many to that path or her ideal political ideology. Further eroding her power grip and traditional bond of destiny it has fostered with the United Kingdom from its inception.

The same United Kingdom alongside America sell hardware to Saudi Arabia to bomb and destroy Yemen, displacing many of its citizens across the world, the same situation that have happened in Syria. It's Hypocrisy for any Nation in Europe to talk about break up or that the migrant crisis is threatening the unity of Europe. How could that be? Apart from Germany, Sweden, Italy and Greece at the frontier, even though most refugees in Greece are unintegrated and socially estranged while neglected to wallow in squalor even selling their bodies for sex in return for money in the streets of Athens, as other parts of Europe have refused to take them in. These are just the few that have recently taken in more people, other countries in Europe are virtually not doing much to help in the situation. Why then, should Hungary that have closed its borders with fences and wires to migrants from the middle easterners, or any other nation complain of the effect's migration has on their unity or culture. Perhaps, borrowing a cue from Spain border wall fences built several years ago to keep migrants through Morocco out from invading their country, where they are not wanted including the rest of Europe.

Trump visited the United Kingdom on July 12, 2018 on a working visit, and during a Press interview he lamented, saying, "Europe is losing its culture and fabric to illegal migration. I don't mean that in a positive way...." he added. Though, he was resisted by the people who came out in droves in tens of thousands across England to rebuke him with placards showing words such as RACIST, BUMBACLAT. Don't forget a giant blimp Trump Baby Balloon was made, approved and flown over London just to show his childishness and ignorance in everything he does. Come to think of it, what is it about the 'Culture of Europe' that would warrant racism and prejudice from Donald Trump targeting agonizing migrants and sowing seeds of discord and unrest all over Europe. He's stoking fires in European domestic policy while stirring up and empowering right-wing groups and white nationalists in Europe like the 'Britain First' extreme and right-wing nationalistic group just like it's in America. In America, the election of Donald Trump to the White House has been cited as a factor in the reemergence of activities and groups in America that reject both left wing ideology and main stream conservatism. Some of them use social media to spread their hate. A United States civil rights group, Southern Poverty Law Center says it tracks about 1,600 extremists' groups within the country. The Alternative Right or alt-right is a group of people who provoke dissent and hate political correctness, and love Mr. Trump, while some of them are bigoted white nationalists. This movement recent rise was encouraged by the rhetoric employed by Donald Trump who was accused of "Textbook Racism," Anti-Semitism and anti-Muslim bigotry. Furthered by the media plat form Breitbart, the movement's ideal focus is on white identity and the preservation of traditional western civilization, according to Richard Bertrand Spencer, who coined the term 'alternative right' in 2008.

Liberty, free speech and the right to offend others who are not tailored to their mindset are its touchstones. Opponents on the other hand call it racist, misogynistic and anti Semitic. They use their online platform especially Breitbart to spread their extreme views towards immigration within their country and in Europe. A political tool that support populist candidates from England, France, Austria to Italy, as they echo the tirade of Trump against migrants and the adulteration of European culture. Donald Trump re-energized Ku Klux Klan in America, a group that historically held extreme right and racist views against Blacks of that country as they have called for the purification of American society as white supremacist. They were established group of racists who believe the whites were better and wanted the Black people to remain slaves. They hate Jews, Roman Catholic, African Americans and recently were opposed to all foreigners into their country as long as they weren't white. There are many others such as the neo-Nazi groups that have sprung up since the election of America's Trump empowered by his racist's tweets based ethnic and religious bias against others. He had made disparaging remarks against women in his country and launched unceasing attacks on Angela Merkel for supporting migration to her country.

The German people that has taken in more of the share are not complaining and reporting more surpluses on yearly basis. Though they would never give any credit to the coming of the migrants into their country as part of the reason the country gets even stronger. The economy thrives locally as it does abroad with exports to countries like America and China. And would still do much more, if not for the division that keeps brewing in Germany by selfish politicians with impact felt in the administration as well as dampening of the authority and influence of the German Chancellor, at home and abroad, knowing when she's weak they'll take advantage of it to further their agenda of bigotry, prejudice and hate to undermine her conservative liberal base in order to succeed her even as they deride other multinationals of other cultures and religions that are different from theirs. All thanks to the Christian Social Union, the upsetting sister party of the Chancellor's Christian Democratic Union led by the demagogue and provocateur Horst Seehofer, who knowing or just realizing their power, wants to shut down the southern border to send a message to the country leader Angela Merkel. Maybe, telling her out rightly, 'it's time to go.' Thinking without their coalition, she might be weakened, and might eventually set in motion another election, if she doesn't find another party coalition to bud with, and such an election might mean she will definitely fail, or so they think. It was reported in the Media that the German spy chief, Maaßen, claimed his agency can't evidently prove that foreigners in Chemnitz were 'hunted' down by the German Neo Nazi rioters, a term Her boss Angela Merkel used after event. After a stormy executive meeting he was absolved by the

Interior demagogue, Seehofer, promoting him as his deputy, regardless of the public outrage captured by all Press and Media houses. The worst is that Angela Merkel couldn't say a word, making her fellow citizens to feel as if she's not in command anymore. She's practically boxed up to a corner, weakened, said some angry youth party coalition members.

This is because the poisoned politics now and the direction of things doesn't favour their deranged policies anymore. Her open-door policy for migrants, and not doing enough to deport illegal migrants, those registered in other first port of entry or those rejected asylum in their country. The Christian Socialists issues are many, and although it seemed as if they are one or support the German Chancellor Angela Merkel in the issues that give her a better world standing, they don't. If it's in their power, she should have been gone after her second or third term. I have been in this part of the country now for a couple of years, I have never heard credit given to her for the unprecedented growth her country has witnessed for the almost two decades she's been in power. But again, one might argue that is the way of many Germans who complements one, on one hand and will always have BUT at the end of the phrase. One might think, this conservative political party's role model is Donald Trump, the world most powerful man and worst role model, redesigning the world order and all the negativity and abuses associated with him. In my understanding, since Angela Merkel took over the country's seat of power and steering the economy, things had progressed from one higher level to another. Germany is now a very rich country and have so much to spend as a result of their surpluses. Like one foreigner in Southern Germany puts it, there are jobs everywhere in this country.

Italy impacted by the rise and demagoguery of Donald Trump could only babble, but have they ever asked themselves: "why refugees go around the streets of Italy begging for money in that country and not in Germany?" Or why asylum seekers flee immediately they disembark from their boats running to Germany, Sweden and other benign European states? It all strengthens my earlier point. Apart from the fact that they detest the sight of refugees on their streets as infestation even though they didn't have a chance to say anything before now until recently when it was rumoured refugees were shot in Italy because it was alleged a Nigerian refugee killed an Italian. Causing an extreme radical to open fire on innocent migrants on the streets of Italy. An inflamed situation that tensed the debates in Italy having many Italian citizens calling for the Migrants to be sent back to their countries of origin because they are spoiling their country. More than ever the recent populist election of the party that brought the current Prime Minister Giuseppe Conte and Interior Minister Matteo Salvini to power riding on the back of populism which they helped to incite in Italy, as many detested and socially estranged migrants end up not having jobs nor integrated in that country neither set on the path of obtaining their citizenship.

All their leaders do is complained, when they really don't offer the real help wanted by refugees, which is to become parts and parcel of their society by being granted asylum and made to eventually socially and culturally integrate into their country for long-term. It's nonsensical hypocrisy. it's a case that can be compared to the French and British imperial colonialists who governed over much of Africa, ruling over what they didn't really like.

If they accept refugees or migrants on the coast and are not prepared to integrate them with the mind of training them, putting them in the labour sector and granting them a stay, which means they have an ulterior motive of throwing those migrants out at any time of their comfort or convenience. Just as they recently called for the deportation of over 500,000 migrants in Italy. Is that even possible? Or, "is it the ramblings of a deranged politician?" Why do the European union decide to take this path? It just came onto them while they least expected it. Once again, its nature taking its course and they are scrambling on how to make it right by them while showing a human face for the world to see.

Now, let's take a look at the United States neighbors, what's going on there and the fundamental reasons triggering the flow of migration from that end. Violence and rampant crime had driven asylum seekers from El Salvado, Guatemala and Honduras to the United States. Tens of thousands of El Salvadorians, Guatemalans and Hondurans, many of them unaccompanied minors, have arrived in the United States in recent years seeking asylum protection from the region's skyrocketing violence. That region was rocked by civil war in the 1980s, leaving a legacy of violence and fragile institutions. The region is plagued by problems such as gang violence, drug trafficking and corruption despite tough reforms and police presence. While the United States may have provided these countries with aid worth billions over the past decade, as long as the regions super power doesn't play an active role to ensure peace and prosperity reigns, that money could go down the drain. But more than ever the United States of America immigration policies in recent times had helped to put fire in to situation as many deported back joins or are forced to join these gangs, a situation that does no good to the country neither United States itself.

The number of Asylum seekers worldwide originating from these three countries reached 110,000 in 2015, a five-fold increase from 2012. It's reported that unaccompanied minors accounted for much of this surge. Migrants from these three South American nations reports forced gang recruitment and extortion, violence as well as poverty and lack of employment opportunity, as their reasons for leaving. While Belize, Nicaragua, Costa Rica and Panama have reported a sharp increase in flows from those of the Northern triangle earlier mentioned since 2008, most migrants pass through to settle in the United States. In 2015, the latest research shows that as many as 3.4 million people born in El Salvado, Guatemala and Honduras were living in the United States. More than double the estimated 1.5 million people in year 2000. About 55 percent of them are undocumented. El Salvado, Guatemala and Honduras rank among the most violent countries in the world. El Salvado became the most violent country not at war in 2015, when gang related violence brought its homicide rate to 103 per 100 thousand. It has since fallen by one third. All the three countries have higher homicide rates than neighbouring Costa Rica, Nicaragua and Panama. Extortion is also rampant as a 2015 investigation shows that Salvadorians and Hondurans pay an estimated 350 million and 200 million and 61 million dollars respectively in annual extortion fees to organized crime groups.

Extortionists primarily target public transportation operators, small businesses, and residents of poor neighborhoods, according to the report, and attacks on those who don't pay or contribute to the violence.

The causes are not far fetched, as the nature of the violence is distinct in each country but the proliferation of gangs, narcotic trafficking, weak rule of law and official corruption are common threads. Organized Crime is a legacy of decades of war in the making over this region, notes a CFR special report.

Criminal groups in these three nations includes trans national criminal organizations, many of which are associated with Mexican drug trafficking organizations, domestic organized crime groups, transnational gangs or Maras such as the Mara Salvatrucha or MS-13 and the 18th street gang or M-18 and other street gangs called Pandillas. The MS 13 and M18 are the regions largest gangs, estimated to have at least 85,000 members in total. Both were formed in Los Angeles. M-18 in the 1960s and MS-13 in the 1980s by Salvadorans who had fled the civil war. Their presence in Central America had grown since the mid 1990s following large scale deportations from the United States of undocumented migrants with criminal records. The Federal Bureau of Investigation estimates there are ten thousand MS-13 members in the United States. Drug trafficking adds to the problem as the U.S. led interdiction efforts in Columbia, Mexico and the Caribbean have pushed trafficking routes to Central America, and the US officials report that 90 percent of documented cocaine flows into the United States now pass through the region. In addition to the drug trade, extortion, criminal groups in the region, they also profit from kidnapping for ransom and human trafficking and smuggling.

Recent United States of America administrations have responded to the violence in the Northern triangle countries in different ways according to reports. George W. Bush focused in fostering the region's growth and stability by increasing trade and introducing free market reforms. Through the Millennium Challenge Corporations, his administrations awarded hundreds of Millions of dollars in grants to Honduras, Nicaragua and El Salvador. In 2005, rising crime rates in central America and Mexico led to a surge of migrants coming to the United States. In response, the Bush's administration introduced a zero-tolerance policy under which migrants illegally crossing the US-Mexico border were criminally prosecuted and deported. In his final days in office, the Bush administration introduced a security assistance package for the region known as the Merida Initiative.

President Obama separated Mexico from the Merida grouping and rebranded it, the Central America regional security initiative (CARSI). Over the years it's reported that the United States have provided more than one billion in aid through CARSI to help the region's law enforcement, counter narcotics, and Justice systems. Midway through his second term, Obama upped the United States policy, forging what was intended to be a more holistic interagency approach. This strategy had three objectives: Promoting prosperity and regional integration, strengthening governance and improving security. The problem with this approach is that America of all should know that aid doesn't always help the people. It mostly goes into the coffers of international agencies and the government. What about the policy of financial and economic investments and training of the youths, as well as helping to make peace between the organized gangs and the government, while supporting the gangs with alternative business approaches. In 2016, amid the rush of arrivals from central America, President Obama ordered the rounding up and deportations of recently arrived migrants whose asylum claims have been denied. The administration said its aim was to deter would be migrants. President Trump has adopted some of his predecessor's approach to the region but has taken a much harder line on immigration policies, including those that affect Central Americans. In line with their new tough policy enforced by the Immigration and Customs Enforcement Agency (ICE), in the near future if not countered, 350,000 immigrants from the Northern Triangle countries could lose the legal right to live and work in the United States as a result of Trump revoking their temporary protected Status, a designation granted to immigrants from countries that have suffered severe hardships. Trump is also expanding the construction of a Border Wall along the USA southwestern border, and his administration has implemented several policies intended to deter migrants from seeking asylum or illegally crossing the border, including criminally prosecuting all undocumented entrants and separating migrant parents from their minor children.

Trump administration separated some 2,500 or more children from their parents, before ending the practice in June 2018, following a national and international outcry. Even though it's reported that migrants or attempted migrants crossing had in the past year decreased up to 26 %.

Americans young and old took to the streets on the 30th June 2018 in America to protest with the message Families belong together, a rebuke of America's Trump policy of separating migrants from their children at the border. The main rally was in Washington D.C., but there were protests in New York, Atlanta, Los Angeles and Houston, calling for an end to family detentions, separations and reformation of the whole immigration policy of the United States to fulfill its true purpose reflecting the true image of America as the land of the free where people who flee rape, violence and persecutions are protected in America and are not sent back, and demanding due process be followed when dealing with the migrant situation as obtained internationally. These events had many speaking their hearts out ranging from those migrants that have experienced such situations before as being separated from their parents with no word from them to American celebrities who voiced their concern to the direction their country was going including politicians from the democratic party, making it clear that America belongs to everyone of them and not their President who's presently out of touch with reality by enforcing policies that go against their ideals of unity in diversity or what the united States had stood for, for centuries.

This would not be the first time Americans are protesting under Trump as the space for protest shrinks on daily basis as Trump over sees an increasing crackdown on activism and dissent, the very thing their leaders accuse other dictators of doing. Over a hundred people still face charges over their alleged involvement in Anti Trump protests on inauguration Day as some might face up to 10 years in jail or a fine of 25,000 dollars. It goes hand in hand with the way folks across the United States of America have been treated as many are repressed from the Standing rock to the pipeline projects, up to the women's right or 'Me Too' movement protest, to the protests by the Black or African American minority against the Trump backed White Supremacists and the authorities mostly the law enforcement culture of impunity over the killings of the young black males, for little or no offense. Free speech under Trump America is witnessing a dearth. But free speech is deeply ingrained in the political and social fabric of that country, and people against all odds will continue to raise their voices in protest against any perceived form of immoral or tyrant culture.

It's hostility towards the first Amendment. In other instances, Trump had lashed out at demonstrators. In February 3, 2017, after a rally against a speech by right wing provocateur Milo Yiannopoulos at the University of California, Berkeley, the President lambasted calling them professional anarchists, thugs and paid protesters. In September 15, of that year protest erupted in St. Louis, Missouri over the acquittal of Jason Stockley, a white former Police officer who shot dead 24 years old Anthony Lamar Smith, an unarmed African American man, nearly six years earlier. Protest spanned weeks. During the first 18 days, Police arrested at least 307 people, as reported by St. Louis Police department. The mass arrests and forceful response to the demonstrations show that criticisms from activists and rights groups, including the American civil liberties union is not tolerated. With an outcry, Trump remained silent on the protests in St. Louis commenting neither on the activities of the Police or the Protests. The constitutional protection that affords people in that country the right to free speech and assembly, among others is eroded. His signal is that free speech isn't his value, and neither should it be that of America a whole. This includes law enforcement and policy makers helping to break this valued or cherished attribute of the land of the free. According to records, throughout Trump's first year in office, right wing state legislators introduced dozens of bills designed to curb the activities of demonstrators in 20 American states. Among them, North Dakota, Oklahoma and Tennessee have passed such bills.

Therefore, the wave of crack down on free speech part by the prosecutors, law enforcement and political forces is a thing of concern on the part of the citizens of that great nation aimed at silencing people, and it should worry the world and all those who see America as the Candle in the Night or the City on a Hill. The nation needs to take a look at itself on a mirror and see whether it reflects those values and principles it so much asks from others and correct itself. Recent spades of protests prompting arrests, killings, hunger and mass migration in Venezuela and the Dictator Daniel Ortega Nicaragua arrests, crackdowns and hundreds of civilian deaths based on his recent social security policy in 2018, should have a powerful and moral voice like that of America urging them to stand down or change their ways. But when it is doing the same things as others and not to mention subjecting asylum seekers into criminal prosecution with tracker chains on their legs and slammed to high security prisons for innocent people fleeing poverty and violence to seek a better life, then it should give the world a pause to rethink and call that country to order. But how could they and in what shape can they achieve that when America's Trump is threatening everyone including his allies with tariffs and withdrawing from international conventions as well as tearing up treaties that keep the order and peace of the world, including pulling out of the Human right organizations, Paris climate accord and even violating the standards of the international labour organization as he withdraws from Trans-Pacific Trade Partnership agreement, a free trade treaty that would liberalize trade and investment between twelve Pacific-rim countries. He rolls back what he calls terrible Obama United States-Cuba cooperative policy. He launches scalding attacks on the organized Media calling them 'Fake Media,' while calling Haiti and Africa detestable names such as "Shithole" due to how he feels about their migration into his country. He does what he pleases and when he pleases without recourse to consequences it will have on others or the stability of the world. If that's not the activities of a raving confusionist and repressive authoritarian who creates an enabling environment for intolerance, hate and far right views to thrive from a world that was once the Bastion of Hope and dreams for immigrants, then tell me what it is?

CHAPTER SIX

TERRORISM AND CULTURAL COMPLEXITIES OF ADAPTING IN GERMANY

So much is talked about migrants and terrorism and their tendency to be involved in terrorists acts and to commit crimes in Germany than the ordinary German citizen. If there's anything agreed by the authorities in Germany as at the time I'm writing this part of the book on July 16th, 2018, is that crime is low, and terrorists' activities are down. What then would a politician, journalist or Political party in Germany such the 'Alternative for Deutschland' and 'Christian Social Union' frame up to be the deciding factor for their brisk political stirring views, state of anxiety informing their vigorous delirious hysteria over poor migrants as they consider them misfits around their streets bashing their already traumatic, disquieting and harrowing mental and physical damage caused by their endurance of excruciating violence, persecution and exploitation while making their journey to Europe. What propels their extreme retroactive laws, policies and regulations strangulating the air of freedom of migrants and refugees within their country while enforcing rejections and forced removals from their country? "Or what factor informs the reasons why especially those politicians in the Southern part of Germany think they've had it to the brim, and they are not taking it anymore?"

I wonder why are statistics not collated of the number of Syrians, Middle Easterners and Africans that exist peacefully and mutually in social bonds with fellow German people? "What's all the fuss about Refugees and Asylum seekers?" Why is there so much emphasis on the migration that took place since 2015 and its perceived negative effects on their land, and nothing good associated with it. Above all, since then the German export economy grew at an all time high in 2016. In 2017, it grew 2.3 percent exceeding the average growth rate of the last ten years with a projection of

2.5 % in 2018. The jobless rate is at all time low, wages are rising, and the public debt clock began winding backwards. "Why is the question of migration to Germany not used to judge the positive effects of the German economic facts and figures?" Why is migration rather often used to judge the German Chancellor Angela Merkel as her point of weakness, hinging it to her inability to win her fourth term general elections out rightly nor secure a coalition with favourable terms than the one she entered into a deal with, whose recent outbursts show that they are nothing more than ethnocentric law and policy makers sitting on the opposite side of the table on important defining issues.

It is largely based on propaganda echoing that the German voters or German people worry about insecurity and crime after allowing in more than a million people in 2015-2016. A sense of guilt is thrown at the Chancellor to correct the mistakes she made by allowing refugees into her country by addressing the security concerns of her people, and to fix the cracks on her vulnerable coalition. This situation, they said could usher in public order.

First, that is inaccurate. There's no public chaos or rampant crime due mainly to the presence of the migrants and refugees in Germany. They've never been. The issue of migration, fear of terror and deepening crime was brought to the forefront by saboteurs in the opposite right-wing parties to discredit her and ensure she didn't win the elections into her fourth term. Angela Merkel administration on her part did a disservice to herself by not sensitizing the German general public of the positive effects the migration has had on their social and economic rich and diverse wellbeing citing precedents from the past. If there's anything happening currently in Germany, is that there's a growing sense of unity in diversity among many of its young and middle-aged population who are gradually getting to share and understanding the foreigners in their classrooms, workplace and in social gatherings even as neighbours in a mutual, harmonious and reciprocal manner. A situation which should be cherished and encouraged in any country in order to make its land and people progressive at an early age by learning to coexist, live with and work with others who don't look like, think or act like them. By finding a balance among that state the country of Germany is in, makes it the more interesting for the country to continue to be what it's always been in terms of demographic inclusiveness and liberal democracy.

The political parties and extreme groups still cite instances of the incident of mass groping and sexual attacks on young women at the New Year's Eve celebrations in Cologne and other cities as an example. There were reported series of terrorist's attacks followed in the summer of 2016, some committed by asylum seekers sympathizers of Islamic State.

Some of which includes, a Patient who fatally injured his doctor before turning the gun on himself at a hospital in Berlin on Tuesday, July 26th, 2016. On Sunday July 24th, 2016 a failed asylum seeker blew himself up outside a wine bar near a musical festival in the German town of Ansbach at about 10.30p.m. The explosion which injured twelve people was the fourth bloody attack in a traumatic week in Germany. There was a Machete attack on Sunday July 24th, 2016 as a Machete wielding Syrian refugee hacked a woman to death in the German city of Reutlingen on Sunday July 24. The man also wounded other two people before a BMW ran him over in the street at about 3.30 p.m. Also, a Gunman named Ali David Sonboly, 18 years old, killed seven teenagers and two adults during a rampage at a Munich shooting centre on Friday July 22nd, 2016. A German of Iranian decent hero worshiped neo Nazi Breivik and launched his attack on the fifth anniversary of the Norway bloodbath. Then, there was the Knife attack on May 10th, 2016, in which a knife man killed a passenger and injured several others during a rampage in a train station in the Bavarian town of Grafing near Munich. The attacker was caught near the station entrance and taken into custody.

Authorities said he was mentally ill and had no proven links to Islamic terrorism.

Additionally, in the fall of that same year in December 2016, there was the Berlin Christmas attack, in which twelve died, exposing massive failings by politicians and the Police. Several of these attackers, if not all have been proven not to have links to Islamic State in the Middle East and were operating with a rash and unstable emotions associated with the trauma and bitter experiences many of them have faced firsthand. Many newspapers reporting an increase in male asylum seekers and refugees involved in killings, rapes and thefts. A situation that caused the Alternative for Germany to coin a term "Criminal Foreigner" to refer to migrants firmly cemented in public discourse in 2017, which according to survey contributed to the rise of the extreme right party called AfD in the Bundestag. They could use different excuses for their rise to power in the German Parliament but their excuse for foreigner's criminal actions in their country as the reason why this extreme right winged party rose to power is a not an intelligent strategy and couldn't have by no means cause their rise to power, if not that they stoke smoke and fire for political gain in circumstances where it's nothing more than fine breathing air.

To start with, long before 2015, they have been the constant rise of hate groups like the Neo Nazi wanting to break out, who particularly were bigoted with their fascist attacks on migrants and foreigners on the rise. Not just about the foreigners but also for the fact that they want to bring back the old ways of Fuhrer Adolph Hitler into a new system and a modern Germany whose thinking has since evolved. They want the old ways of racism, discrimination, sexism, xenophobia and narcissism brought back not just as a way to treat foreigners who have helped to develop the German economy but to institute it to limit the freedom of its own people in going liberal and progressive. There have been several reports of attacks meted on foreign immigrants especially Africans long before 2015, as such elements or Germans with such extreme beliefs in public service implement their racists ideology to discriminate against foreigners even though these foreigners were born here, and some have been naturalized in Germany, and could communicate in their language very well. There was an instance of a migrant in East Germany who reported attacks on him by extreme locals living around his area, a dark episode he had to relive every day, not only mentally but physically as those people pick up on him due to his looks and the way he speaks Germany, to harass and torment him almost on daily basis even with physical abuse.

This situation was common after the 2015 mass migration to Germany as many hostels were set alight and suspected migrants and refugees not allowed to participate or enter into public social gatherings, parties or clubbing. That is the starting point of extreme party organizations such the Alternative for Deutschland solidly cemented in the Bundestag. It's obvious the only thing holding such parties and their members in the German Parliament from arresting and putting all migrants and refugees in holding centres, deporting hundreds of thousands and rejecting further refugees into their country is the law. But each day we have seen how this narrow mindedness, and judgmental even prejudiced behavior tends to shift the grounds of the receptivity of the laws and rules put in place by the European union and Dublin convention to ensure migrants are treated humanely and accorded the due freedom which they deserve, which even Angela Merkel described to the eurocentric, egocentric, chauvinist and bigoted Hungary's Prime Minister Victor Orban, as 'the Soul of the European Union.' "If these people in the German Bundestag are not fascists 'Germany First,' oppressing, sectarian Neo Nazis fatherland fighters in collected suits and beautiful looks, elected to positions of power to legislate for the good or socio-economic welfare of Germans, thinking they have good intentions and the good of the country at heart, then tell me who the are?" If such ideas or hard line conceptions as held by these politicians are implemented, does any German think it will lead to a peaceful society and healthy economy, after these hundreds of thousands of people have been here for years already and in one way or the other contributed to the rising economic miracle growth of the Republic of Germany are rounded up and deported. This, by the way, couldn't have been the fault of the asylum seekers but because the German authorities whose arms of government are shared by the right wing parties have decided not to give them a legal stay or allow them recognition and the social status they seek in order to integrate and be productive residents of Germany like any other person born in the country is allowed to.

Of course not, if history has anything to teach these people is that the end of all these bickering and division would only lead to a decline or deterioration of the activity within the economy, and then everyone would suffer the penalty. Then, the situation or complain would be rather serious as it would lead to a break down in law and civil order as every citizen would complain how the economy is doing bad, and why those in power should be out. By then, their phrase would definitely be that it's the migrants and refugees that caused the stagnation in the economy because they've usurped all the jobs and vacancies. They'll say because of Angela Merkel's open door policy, the country is ruined and the economy has tanked, and we should blame the poor refugees as scape goats for their seemly downward spiral in a tide of migration that has more positive sides than its opposite including contributing to the growth of the economy from within to a fair, rational and welcoming image posterior of Germany from the outside.

"It's most definitely going to occur," a situation, they themselves brought to the country by their lack of unity or ability to be united in an issue such as immigration and to create awareness of how migration has helped the people and economy rather than the contrary. A situation even the current German Chancellor Angela Merkel is failing deeply in exercising. Maybe by the time, she thinks of that light of approach, the opportunity may no longer be there. This was the same situation that happened in the United Kingdom during the leave Europe Referendum and campaign, as the former Prime Minister David Cameron today has regretted not informing or carrying a campaign on awareness to inform the public on what such radical approach of separating from Europe due primarily to migration would cost his country including the positive effects of migration in his country. Today, the government and its many supporters are in a fix as some has regretted such decision and fear shame instead of reversing back to a united Europe. Especially since the new policies of America which they thought were allies are beginning to present a very clear reality and present dangers associated with leaving Europe and cutting down on migration flow. Whether the migration comes from Asia, Eastern Europe, Middle East or from Africa, it's called Migration, and its effects, if well managed, according to history and general survey leads to consequent growth and boost in the economy other than a burden.

Now Angela Merkel has the same opportunity to educate his people on the positive effects of migration, a situation that cost Prime minister Cameron of Britain his position, and may likely do more than take away her party's dominance in the Parliament by the presidency ultimately losing to a party whose standards and touchstones are in stark contrast to her own and that of her party, the Christian Democratic Union. If that situation happens, in the long term, I bet it will not only be the migrant that might suffer but the German on the street might experience the dark effects of such a terrible mistake. More than ever, their world standing and influence they formerly had as partly leaders of the free world as a result of the face of humanity and love of the country shown to foreigners, as well as power to sway not just Europe to bend to their democratic standards, might be eroded even as they bring disunity and strong views including protests among the very fabric of the society that person was elected to protect.

Recently it's reported that tens of thousands of migrants and failed asylum seekers have vanished from the system. Impossible to say, because of the sheer numbers and the German decentralized federal states, which have their own rules, and methods of collating their figures of refugees and crimes, combined with the chronic inability to communicate with one another, including Berlin. As well as the strict limits on what information the Police can release about crimes, suspects and victims has further complicated issues. This situation has caused the inability for the country to say exactly how many refugees have vanished from their custody including children, as they bother about the issues and problems of migration they think affects them, without the least consideration of the lives and security of those migrants whom they care little about, and if they have them in their grabs, will not hesitate to throw them out. This has been the boon of populists, whose suggestions are subjective, and more concerned about punishing refugees and migrants for data produced by them which is often inaccurate as compared to the hard data on the ground, on their contribution to a diverse country, learning of tolerance by the indigenous population, social unions and the cultural interactions.

Amongst other problems facing a migrant, refugee or a child born in Germany of immigrant background are the complexities of adapting to a new society whom the people think and act different and even look different to them. For the young people or adults coming into this environment and realized that they are discriminated against, it's a scar that stays with them into the future. Some of these foreigners grow up in a society where they experience several restrictions that limit their rights as a person to liberty and social expression even though not publicly stated. A situation where a foreigner or migrant who is middle eastern or African is denied entry to a social gathering, concert or a club, sometimes even with their identity cards in front of them while all others are allowed to stroll into the venue because they look German or European in their appearance, are aspects even though when unspoken or hardly reported, leads to the migrants feeling not at home, rejected and unwanted in their new society.

Or a situation in the classroom, where the teacher knowing fully well there are migrants who have not fully integrated including understanding the language, teach a certain subject as though all the students are on a level playing field. Such a child or adult, getting an education or a job training theoretical studies in any given institution often with Deutsche, the German language might find it difficult to catch up leading to dropouts, as it takes time to get used to a new system, learn in a language which is not native to them that might take forever to know completely, and in subjects or courses that are available to them in their new country which they had no knowledge of, before they got to the country. These are some of the odds stacked against some of these migrants and refugees trying to inculcate into the new system and society, they find themselves in such as Germany

Additionally, the adult refugee or migrant inside Germany amongst many headaches, is still battling his case in courts or the immigration department, as many are refused asylum or sanctuary more times than they could count, and that migrant perhaps still in school, working or like many others unable to find a steady job, or denied the right to employment completely. Such a dormant or confused mind of a person denied job and education but still loitering around the country with no joy of life and mental instability piled up from all his rejections by the government and the social environment that is unfriendly and frustrating, might be prone to releasing his emotions in negative acts such as crime and terrorists acts including destroying himself with decisions to a lifestyle that might endanger his life and health with long-term consequences. For one person, among hundreds of thousands who readily feel they could be deported anytime out of the country into the very life they have fled from, such pain accruing from not being wanted in Germany, Italy or Sweden, might in the long-term have adverse consequences on the host country including the formation of gangs or cult groups initiations with an extreme ideology that might come back to bite the government and their people, the same thing they are trying to avoid, all resulting from a mind that is not properly used, as a result of the cruel policies of the extreme right winged politicians who don't consider others but themselves.

Therefore, action might be needed on this part by the government and although the current government is facing challenges largely linked to migration, their inability to be unified in their action to act to give migrants true freedom, especially the freedom linked to the right of stay and integration in their new country by regularizing their status to a long-term one, giving hope to this agony stricken foreigners, one might pose a danger that might outstrip what ever challenges that are currently faced by the current administration of Angela Merkel and her opposition in the government.

It's easy to say, deport them. Send them all back. But some of these people are already determined to stay here or kill themselves in the process of fighting for such human rights. All Angela Merkel is fighting for, some believe, is for the rights of the asylum seekers to come inside her country even though they are registered in their first port of entry into Europe but what she fails to realize is that, those measures are inadequate. In order to make her efforts established or long-term, she must advocate or lobby her opposition, for many of those already in her country marked for deportation to be allowed to stay. That is the main issue. Whatever made these foreigners leave their homeland, isn't suddenly disappeared. The problems of wars, violence and poverty persists. Not the other aspect of allowing people to come inside her country when she knows that after all they might be rejected in the end and sent back to their country of nativity. But how could she even suggest such a thing when she is surrounded by wicked allies whom she claims to be friends, who are actually stabbing her at the back everywhere she goes.

But even though she is surrounded by haters for her open-door policy, and opponents who want her out of power at every turn and would like to take advantage of every loophole to further their hate agenda for migrants, why couldn't she just do what is necessary, and care less of what her opposition members think and might help her country in the long-term. Statistics as at 2017, show that over three hundred thousand people were rejected asylum, some of which are still active in the society. If she takes a dare at helping them by aligning herself with the fair minded and centre left members in her party and coalition as well as appealing to the generality of the German populace through paid adverts for the people to see the positive side of migration, that might help her to boost her support from the people, while pushing back the extremists in the government including the hardline views of legislators or neo-Nazi look alike in the Parliament and the executive arm who want to see her fall, at any given opportunity and to wipe out her gains and good reputation, just like Trump did to Barack Obama in America. Yes, the migrant children contribute to the growth of the economy and are the future of the country if they are well educated, integrated or assimilated into the system, but then there are others.

The adult population of migrants and asylum seekers far outstrips that of children in Germany, as these people are thinking adults who made a logical decision to leave their countries to Europe in search for a better life. Such a mindset when encouraged, as the government see ways to which these people are granted a legal status or offered a legal path to citizenship in the long-term, those very adults will perform and even exceed expectations as they are hungry for success more than the German who's born here.

Others within Europe look at Germany as an example for them to follow, and even though they are threats of division and breakup within the Union, if the migration issues are not well tackled. The truth is, they wouldn't leave because the benefits of them staying far outstrips their leaving the Union. More also, there is the rise in populism to oppose Angela Merkel in the European Union by new governments in Europe who are on the far right, and seeing the dark effects of having backward migrants in their land, who are not ever having hope of being accepted in the system, which domino effects creates problems like crimes and fuel gang related crimes like in Italy, making the people wanting them out or deported. In Germany, it's not the same case as the country has a system that is unique and different from Italy or Greece and takes care of its own people in its custody even allowing them to a certain degree to be integrated into the system through education and jobs which are readily available, unlike in Italy. Therefore, if the present administration of Angela Merkel think they might escape the issue of migration, it's self deception. This issue will characterize the future of that administration and the direction of the government even in the foreseeable future. Knowing this fact, like it's debated in America, why can't the government create a solid legacy not based on fear of their opponents but the pride of accepting the righteousness in their actions even as they sensitize the public on the necessary light that might come from this decision of providing a path to legal status or residence for all the many people they accepted to take into Germany, and who have been here now for several years. As well as the need to ensure its integrity is shaped on the spirit of liberalism and humanity it offers to the anguished migrants by letting them integrate into the social fabric of his country instead of following the rules of the European convention, which they themselves break to deport the migrants, even though individual evidence to the above show otherwise.

Additionally, this approach is not a favour to the refugees and migrants but done for the good and long-term stable future of the country. Knowing it's a proud legacy not of shame or disappointment, should energize the leaders, not only this path, but as well as introducing other executive and legislative policies that affects every foreigner in German positively, to feel welcome and act as responsible residents of their new land, they call home. These includes policies that affect their education, encourage social integration, as well as cultural sharing and interaction of those already granted asylum but feel estranged, and saying, "And now what?" If Angela Merkel who had excelled in all areas and bringing their country into a period of plenty, now before she goes out of power, does the right thing that might benefit the least recognized or alienated in the society, history will judge her in the true light, as a leader who didn't budge even in pressure in the face of a strong opposition. But thinking she and her administration could take the easy way out and bow to pressure by harkening to the dictates of the plotters of her down fall and critics within and outside, who might later use her as an example to justify their actions of dehumanizing the humanity of immigrants, migrants and refugees on their shores, will be a grave mistake. It will only spell misery, confusion and sense of unfulfillment for her as she risks wiping out all her gains as well as respect she earned around the world by that honorable step she took by granting sanctuary to refugees fleeing war, violence, hunger and danger in this sensitive subject which everyone knows the right thing to do.

CHAPTER SEVEN

EXTREME REALITY OF REFUGEE MIGRATION TO GERMANY

Many writers and analysts have written about Germany as a model society and inclusive country with a good legal, social and economic system. Among other merits of living in the country are the good infrastructures and stable economy. The country has the sovereignty of law over all and protection for all, some describes it as its biggest and valued strengths. Others say law and order, safety of life and protection of property, gender equality and a modern society, all made Germany one of the best countries' in the world to live in. "Sensible laws and an open society" came out on top among respondents, who reacted on social media to prove Germany is a good country to live in.

Secondly, the Good transport infrastructure: The country has good inter and intra city trains and trams that made it easier to get around the Bundes Republic. The accessibility of trains to travel from one city to another as well as Metro trains that are functional and up to date and are readily available in minutes for commuters to use them to go from one point to another makes it a viable country to attract tourists to every part of its country to see historical sites. Others claim being able to walk from their homes to a bakery or coffee shop or supermarket makes it worthwhile. Also, driving being a good experience in Germany with cautious, courteous, and skillful drivers and an excellent autobahn system. Not forgetting the country boasting of having some of the best roads in the world.

Thirdly affordable Health care: Germany's health-care system works largely with public health insurance schemes. So, the sickness or disease one is suffering from is covered by the health care insurance and be sure that you will be treated free of charge in the hospital without additional financial burden or won't have to beg to foot the bills.

Fourth, the people and social life: Some reported survey find Germans to be great and lovely people filled with personality. They have great food and good people, and everyone is friendly. Awesome beer. Food is cheap. Basic household goods are cheap and great bread in the world. Because the economy is good, people have disposable income to travel. The people support their diverse and all-inclusive football teams and are open minded people. They have different social groups funded by the government and other companies that takes care of the needs of the people and makes people to belong other than being alone. Also, such social groups provide education to people to ensure people are educated about any given subject that affects the generality of the people ranging from Race issues, HIV-AIDS to cultural topics. Not forgetting the nightlife that affects thousands each day and mostly on weekends to explore the beauty of looking at the country at another lens including mingling and getting into relationships and mutual friendships. They focus on not just economic success but on time for family, friends and time away from work.

Fifth, Germany is an educated country as it has in place if not the best then it will be one of the best educational system in the world. Primarily everyone is expected to go to school whether his or her parents have money or not such a child have to be educated as it's against the country's law for any child to be uneducated. Apart from its regular educational system from Primary to the University level, the country has since put in place a system of vocational studies where people who are not as brilliant or keen on going to the university or furthering to acquire a high degree of knowledge in the tertiary level could afford themselves the vocational institutional studies where they could be trained on a wide range of professions and skills from mechanic to a Health care provider. It's very effective that most countries now copy from them to improve or make up for their lingering or backward educational system without much opportunities including the United States. This system is responsible for ensuring almost everyone gets a trade or acquires a skill in order to fit into the economic society. A three-year training and practice that ensure the student studies, does his practical, works and he is paid at the same time. it's a dynamic and attractive system to many of the country's youths who don't see themselves going beyond secondary school level of education. But this system is not only for youths but for adult as well, as everyone is entitled to afford his or herself this opportunity to better their life, improve their skill and make a better fortune.

Sixth, the country is diverse and multi cultural as immediately you arrive this country you see a whole range of people from every part of the world living together. Like one African man puts it, the place I stay in Berlin have children and families speak up to 50 languages. It's quite diverse and that makes the country beautiful. The demographic is diverse. They are about 82 million people in that country and 10 million of them hold a foreign passport, more than in any of the 28-member European Union. Berlin is particularly diverse as among the 3.5 million people in that city over a million of them are not originally Germans as they emigrated to that country from about 185 countries of the world. As many as 47 percent of Frankfurt's residents are not German by root as one in 7 companies have foreign background too. So, why the appeal for migration into Germany, some might say is related to opportunities available for personal advancement. Some say, it's the diverse opportunities, good prospects and interesting jobs on offer.

In a survey of 24 countries conducted by BBC world service in 2014, Germany was once again voted the world's most popular place because of lifestyle, high quality products and a successful image.

Practically, all the larger German cities feature a wide mix of nationalities of various nations striving together to make that country great. A melting pot of different cultures, religions, languages and people.

Many people from immigrant background have become highly successful due to the opportunities offered by the country from entrepreneurs to engineers and doctors. Others are employed in skilled labour in industry and restaurant trade. Some go into film and music industry. Even their German football team is representative of that diversity even though Mesut Ozil quits Germany national football team citing racism. "I am a German when we win, and Immigrant when we lose." He added in his post. Moreover, Germany is a place to live and work as many nationalities feel at home as a place to live and raise their kids too. Some of the credit of the nation goes to its political and economic stability and a caring society. More so, it's comprehensive health care system, protection of the rights of minorities and freedom of religion amongst others. Also, the country is one of the most peaceful countries on earth and has seen no major political unrest for several decades now. The lists go on and on for people.

That said, on the reasons why an immigrant or desperate migrant fleeing poverty, war and persecution would prefer Germany to his own country in East Europe, Africa or the Middle East. It's said a good, respectable and humane society is rated or scored based on how it treats those at the bottom of the scale The question is, does the good legal system and open diverse society benefit migrants, asylum seekers and refugees, when this anguish stricken migrants and refugees are slammed and restricted to live, work, if possible and travel only around their location of designation. If that's not abuse of basic freedom by denying a human being in a civilized society the right to travel from one city to another to meet a friend or relative, tell me what it is then? A migrant or asylum seeker located in any given city in Germany is given a specific time to stay in the country with a temporary renewed status of stay. After this period is over, the person is issued a letter compelling him or her to attend an interview in one immigration office or another to state the reasons why they fled their country of birth to Germany as Asylum seekers.

Ask refugees from Eastern Europe, North and West Africa, it's almost basic that your right to asylum will be denied you no matter the grounds or reasons you lay forward, especially under the present highly debated immigration issues and poisoned atmosphere. Mostly based not on those interviewing the applicant or the fault of the asylum seeker but of the law makers and legislators in the Bundestag as their policies dictate which person from what region or country is considered for asylum and not based on a common index for examining and determining a procedure that is sometimes inaccurate.

How many of those law makers have ever conceived of and set up an initiative, to invite a select general groups of Asylum seekers or have this numerous and diverse number of refugees from different countries be represented and come to their Parliament as another avenue of appealing to the good side of the legislators to take action by recounting or telling them their stories firsthand. Maybe, if they got to hear the stories of some of this Asylum seekers from the horse's mouth, of issues pertaining famine, extreme poverty, wars, violence, political repression, torture, rape and religious or ethnic persecution, it might change their thinking, views and calculation with the way they make and put forward new arbitrary retroactive legislation on quarterly or yearly basis to further lead to the detriment or worsen the anguish of mental suffering situation already faced by the many people in the country more than they already do.

After they make sure one is denied asylum, the person is given a status called Duldung or Tolerated status. Under this tolerated status, you are worse off than you were before. Maybe you were allowed to travel around the state or the country but return to your base. Under this new Duldung status, one placed in such a level is restricted from traveling to other places and if allowed, they are warned not to travel beyond three days. Worse off, is that if one was working before under this new status of Duldung, you likely will be forced to stop working whether in any factory, industry or restaurant. Some people are put in this position but are not deported for a long time. How could then one live in a limbo like situation this status puts one into. Mostly crime makes rejected applicants' rate of deportations fast paced at least until now. Who knows what the next laws would have in the future as the regional and national legislative arm are urging rejected applicants to be quickly deported even if they resist deportation or in the midst of protests.

First the judicial and fair legal system is flawed for the common asylum seeker, as under this stringent condition they operate in, other arms of the government including the Judiciary, who formerly were correctors of the misdemeanor or errors of the migration and foreign department, but now are complicit and have no balls to challenge the ruling of the migration department that has refused a stay to an asylum seeker despite his travails and persecution. Sometimes, their judgment or ruling is based on the rule of the safe country system initiated by the national legislature. Where some countries are delineated as being safe and migrants from those countries can return back to them, not taking into consideration the political turmoil, breakdown of rule of law, torture, arrests and breaching of freedom rights of citizens by meting violence, pain and political or religious persecution on these people. So, once again, while, the majority of visiting foreigners or tourists even long time immigrants, cite some interesting aspects of the country that interest them as to why the country is a model to live and work in, they should consider others down the ladder, the migrants and refugees without a voice, who are treated badly with prevailing new rules and regulations to limit or stifle the air out of their sometimes unbalanced mental state, a situation faced by many refugees and asylum seekers from the very day they step into Europe or Germany to the very day they are finally deported from that country.

The same applies to the supposed good transport system. If the migrant and asylum seeker don't move around or can't move to any place of his choice to meets friends and families or are not allowed to due to provisions in the law, then, the benefits of a good transport system to the asylum seeker no matter how long he or she stays in that country, is not effective as he's always watching his or her back while jumping into a bus, car or train to travel to other locations or cities in order to free the mind, body and soul from the prison they are put into. How can they appreciate the beautiful country side or tourists sites when they are not allowed to work or when given the Duldung status, a status on temporary passports that is growing in number even though not officially reported for a country that was never ready to accommodate their foreign migrants to make them truly feel welcome by granting them a stay and frown at any regional authority that does that, says volumes to the friendliness and receptive position of Germany.

In terms of Healthcare, while it may be good or better of for the migrants than it's in their own countries but as an asylum under that protected status one is supposed to be afforded the care or health care he or she needs to stay healthy whether they'll be deported in the end or granted a stay. The problem, with this system is that, the law prohibits an asylum seeker from working, and the applicant is given some certain money to feed. If such a person, suffers from problems not covered by the Healthcare system, such as person is expected without help to come from no place to use the little money he or she is given to pay for that health care service offered to him. For example, a migrant loses a tooth or more. Under the system, the insurance allocated covers the dental health of its people including extraction and artificial replacement. Then, one at some point is expected to pay, and the more choice one has, the more, he or she, without any other sources of income may be expected to scurry from the little he's got to pay for the tooth he or she has lost even though it's install mental payments.

All of these, is added to the same migrant having to pay his lawyer every month for the entire period of his trial or judicial case aimed at getting another point of view or review at his or her case, and if lucky, will be granted a permanent stay in the country which during these times of a politicized debate on this topic, it's highly unlikely unless one originates from those countries the laws or regulations by the National parliament has stipulated that should be granted a stay due to the poor state of their countries, either as a result of war, violence or extreme hunger. There fore, once again, the health care is good but when it comes to the foreign migrant or asylum seeker who need basic health services affecting either his tooth or eyes such as affording a brand-new lens, needed to correct one's sight, after probably surgery, one must pay for himself without subvention from the health care insurance covering them.

The world are told how good the migrants are taken care of but in essence, a migrant that is dumped in a hostel for several years without being sponsored to get education or skill on any job, given a meager sum of money to survive on, with the hope of deporting as many of them as they can, when the given or right environment presents itself, doesn't show much of a loving, beautiful, unprejudiced, fair and reasonable people.

We are told of how nice the people are, and how vibrant the social life in Germany is. Once again, how much of all of this great German story affects the common Asylum seeker or refugee. These people from the very day they land in Germany, they are discriminated against and some even treat them like drags, outcasts or social misfits without respect or show of love. A situation where those in the social department in charge of handing out money think they are doing one a favour, and not being nice while serving the migrant or giving them their social allowance. Or, for example, when there was Ebola in Africa, and those at the foreign office, Caritas or Social department using it as excuse not to be nice or treat the new entrants with love and courtesy they deserve. Or, what about the number of foreign migrants stuffed within a room, sometimes four to six people in a not too large room, living in worst conditions possible with unclean or infected toilets.

Well, that is within the confines of the hostel they are located. But what about outside the confines of where they are housed like in the clubs or a social environment? It's generally agreed Germany like the United Kingdom and other European Nations are difficult places to socialize, make friends and generally integrate into the new environment and with its people. Some foreigners especially refugees are often blamed saying their inability to get a girlfriend or boyfriend is because they are ignorant of the culture of the land. It's true but generally, Germans are people who are very hardworking whose lives in the office or at work is to a large extent streamlined and could be understood. Even to a certain level, some argue that their private and social lives are conditioned due to the liberalized environment they grew up in and the American movies they watch as they grew up.

Therefore, these people conditioned in a certain way on how to operate within a business environment acts exactly the same way as expected of them. But that same person outside his or her office and the veil off, becomes a different person. From the perspective of the foreigner, you'd ask why? But she was nice, attentive and all, inside the office and how come she has changed all of a sudden now you can't easily approach and speak to her. Yes, it's the way the system is made to operate. The same reason why so many Germans look at the traffic light and wait until it's green before they cross or not rob other people's things or not fight in public, at least most of them, is the same exact reason why they behave they way they do while at office or working environment. That is because they fear the consequences, if they don't comply to the instructions or follow those regulations as rolled out by the society. If they break them, they are liable to be punished, sometimes judged in a certain unfriendly way, dismissed from work or arrested if they violate the public rules.

That fear of consequences makes many Germans try to do anything to avoid jail by acting in a law-abiding fashion including not committing a serious, abusive or intentional crime and being careful in their behavior because of the negative social reaction or legal consequences. This makes their jails, not crowded or very few Germans found in prison cells. However, that doesn't include minor stealing, Marijuana and other drugs intake, as it's estimated that most young people or adults at one time or the other had been part of such a juvenile delinquent lifestyle, therefore accounting to the high demand of this illicit trade among the young adult population, mostly blamed on foreigners as the peddlers who are often jailed but the local consumers who demand the product are lightly corrected.

Just like the private lifestyle of many young people in Germany based on their freedom to smoke, drink and drugs intake. They have their social views concerning the migrants and refugees, including maligning or insulting them, if they perceive him or her not to be worth their time. A lot of foreigners or migrants who successfully bond with German men and women in social unions and relationships often complain that they just can't understand them outside sexual consummation. But the truth is, even their people can't understand them. That accounts for the reason why many immigrants and migrants especially the men are alone and isolated often blamed on their lack of understanding or ignorance for the German culture on how to talk to, be friendly and make friends with Germans as well as what's expected of them when reaching out on this regard. It's worse, if that migrant or refugee's status is known or revealed to them, instead of that status helping the person to get a girl or man, it rather turns the emotions to pity, and that's not what the refugee wants. There are lots of Non-governmental organizations doing that work, and another thing a refugee wants, is sympathy and fear from whomever the refugee is attracted to, and more love and sexual passion required.

It's a nightmare for anyone if that happens whether in the local pub or club. That accounts for why many would rather keep their status or identity to themselves as where one comes from could make an interested person, who could have made a close friend, acquaintance or intending sexual partner to change his or her mind over you. It's based on stereotypes given certain people from different countries in Africa making it difficult to exercise their freedom and express themselves freely to get friends or get out of the friend-zone in the social circles, in some cases.

But that has to do with social life. What about the employers of labour? When a migrant is privileged to get a job, he or she is likely not to last in such a job, as his or her inability to speak the German language fluently sometimes makes life difficult for the person as they can't really communicate what they wish to say or seek proper redress when they are offended. A situation where other workers would gather around and gossip whether in working hours or break time, leaves less to be desired. The act of gossip and backbiting pervades every aspect of the German public life. Like, one local put it, I have never seen people who do small talk like the Germans at work. And when one is new as a migrant and get caught up in that web, it will most definitely lead to dismissal as his or her inability to catch up quickly or work as fast as the Germans or communicate effectively, would make them liable to be the point of small talk and amusement of others who ridicule, sometimes making them feel less than human.

Such actions are not just exclusive to migrants alone as the act of backbiting is pervasive. But in more than not, such maleficence doesn't translate to the dismissal or firing of the German citizen such that the effects it has on the migrant's psychological life as each day until he or she is fired, they are pressed to face the same people who humiliate them in words and deeds. Perhaps, it's because of how they look, as a foreigner once put it, even though you're naturalized here as an immigrant especially as a Black man who probably works in the high end level of the business or public sector, you could be denied your rights to leading a company because your colleagues don't like you or have something against you. Not your ability to hard work as that has been tested to get you to where you are but just the fact that you are different from them in your color, could make you ineligible for promotion to assume the top job in a big company. And when you are a refugee and your status is known by other employees, some might take advantage of your status or inability to speak good German language to treat you bad, being nasty or not being decent with you. Sometimes, you hear it straight from the chief of the organization from the very first day, telling you that you don't have a future there. Go to school or vocational training called Ausbildung, to get the training required, that is the only way to secure a future or permanent job, where one isn't kicked out. This emphasizes on the challenges facing an immigrant, migrant or refugee all the way whether in the social circle or at work.

Much is talked about the German educational system as being one of the most successful in the world today. The question is, how does that affect the asylum seeker and migrants in Germany and other benign European states. Yes, it's true that according to the Dublin convention, the children or minor are protected including been offered compulsory education to train their minds to develop to become responsible adults of the society. That said, what about the adult that is within Germany, who is capable of contributing to the society and is a migrant housed in a hostel who came probably because of the bad economic situation in his country, which of course is behind the reason why everyone travels apart from the fact that they suffer from war, persecution and violence. If extreme poverty and hunger is agreed and known by the authorities as the reason why a majority of all refugees, migrants and immigrants travel out of their land, why don't the authorities use that knowledge of the cause driving the migrants as enough motive to train them to become self sufficient and skilled from the very day they step into their land.

Mind you, some of these migrants have stayed in Germany for five to fifteen years fighting waiting to get regularized under a tyrant and oppressive system that don't want them. Now it's agreed Germany has a good system of education with their expanded vocational system of education called Ausbildung. This system like I earlier said accounts for why most Germans are educated, skillful and are employable. This is most definitely the system most of those minors would take advantage of, to excel in their new country. Why not set up a less than narcissistic regulatory system for the refugees where one who's been in the country from three to months at least could begin acquiring such an educational training and skills in any profession they aspire to, in order to get brained up and running, as some people waste out ending up engaging in the unlawful act of drug peddling and other immoral acts widely available in the country.

One could argue that some are allowed to work. Yes, after my arguments earlier, we would realize that such employment opportunity is not effective for the migrant who is just only a matter of time before he or she is being sacked from work after being made fun of. The concept of integration is true if the people allowed in to country even though it's a one-year training is being offered the opportunity to integrate into the normal educational system, after all no man or woman is too old to study and acquire skills. If history has taught us anything, is that most foreigners due to their level of determination excel better than the indigenous population. In no time, they are out, having acquired a skill in life that might help them to excel in life whether they are consequently sent back or let to remain. All these bigoted laws and legislation passed against the welfare of migrants only worsen their situation and in effect, doesn't help anyone neither their host country. So, for example, as an asylum seeker in a hostel, there are many NGO's among which is the Caritas and Sant' Egidio operated by the 'Catholic World' helping to support and ensure the wellbeing of refugees and victims of crisis in Germany and other European Countries.

During the early period of the migrant stay in the hostel, they are treated to daily study of the language knowing well that without the basic understanding of Deutsche language, one may not go far enough. So, they are drilled to ensure they comprehend the basic skills of proper and interpersonal language communication and its importance including listening, speaking, reading and writing. But that's all about it. Under the regulations of asylum, anyone granted a stay or refugee status in Germany automatically qualifies to pursue a program, an official language course with a certificate, and for one to qualify for a permanent stay certification one has to further stay for a certain period between two to three years and then pass at least the B2 certification; spoken and written language test with a score qualifying the regularized refugee, a status like any other German with full rights, a stay certification called "Unbefristet' meaning without limit or permanent stay. And if the person wants to go further, perhaps into the university, one may have to go further and pass a higher test to qualify one to gain admission to a higher education. Otherwise, the B2 certificate is enough to get one into a local school to pursue a vocational educational study called 'Ausbildung', done by most Germans, provided the person has a basic secondary school certificate earned by a school back at home in their country.

That's where it also gets crazy. For one fleeing war and persecution or violence, the last thing he or she remembers to carry is his school certificate or test papers, if they are not already burnt. Why can't the legislature fashion out a special scheme within the traditional institutions for the many refugees and migrants fleeing from their countries to Germany, to be able to go ahead and study in this vocational system or avail themselves a higher education without being asked to provide those basic secondary school papers, from their home country which in many cases doesn't exist because many of those coming across the borders are uneducated. If educated, it's likely for one fleeing war and violence such a certificate might be destroyed by the series of many problems besieging the several unstable and volatile nations in the world, whose people have become refugees even in their own land, and the last thing such a person thinks about is searching and grabbing their certificate as an insurance as they flee their land. Just as it's difficult to get a valid passport and a visa on it during times of war, or as a migrant waiting or cuing for one, in order to flee his or her country, the same applies to this case.

That is, for the stranded adult migrants already granted a stay or refugee status, and are languishing in the system, and couldn't go any further, perhaps getting a proper education in order to be truly integrated into the society. A situation that might help the person refine or improve his or language oral, writing and other skills. But for those other abandoned asylum seekers and migrants in the system already refused asylum by the German authorities, who are in hundreds of thousands across the country, jumping either from one temporary job to another, when allowed to work, such schemes could be useful to them to enable them as human beings, who they are to effectively contribute to the society they now live in, or in the case, of when they are forced to return to their country of origin, if that's a necessary step to take at all.

Therefore, as a note of advice or letter addressed to the Bundestag, the German national parliament and the executive arm. I duly advise that they put all these critical points into consideration, while they make their unbiased, tolerant and liberal legislative laws or open-minded policies affecting innocent refugees and migrants who are only looking for what's best for them and their family away from an environment wrought with war, famine and destruction.

So, with all these salient points of significance and consequence, analyzed and highlighted here, if the necessary framework of logistics and programs are put in place and followed up appropriately, *as work of government and not that of non governmental organizations and aid agencies to enable migrants and refugees to rightly integrate while enhancing their skills effectively to become happier in their new society, as well as proud members of their host communities contributing to the peace, unity and upliftment of the society, it will help to solve or highly reduce the incidents of suicide and psychological breakdown even prolonged cases of mental illnesses experienced by many refugees and migrants exacerbated by the inhumane and unfriendly laws of 'wall over people'* initiated by their host nations on the poor new seekers of refuge while in the country of their dreams.

Please look at this title too from Arikpo Lawrence Omini
Supernatural. Action Adventure. Mythology.

A special boy is led down from the skies. An Ashanti king is born. The one prophesied to change the course of the world and time itself. The leopard king Kwakwu fled after his Kingdom was attacked and his father killed in an odyssey that will eventually prepare him for his future. He returned after completing his thirteen labors in the jungle assigned to him by Selene, Moon Goddess that cursed him with the fabled seventy-two skins of invincibility and great power. He fought and defeated the overlord of the alliance to claim back his throne as King. He was later killed by a lion as was long predicted after he successfully established a futuristic utopian 'World Kingdom,' a new world society ruled by love for the environment, unity in one faith, as well as equality and prosperity for all. A thrilling story, full of adventure, mystery, suspense and intense.

Published and printed by tredition GmbH | www.tredition.de/buchshop

ISBN:
978-3-7469-4086-1 (Paperback)
978-3-7469-4087-8 (Hardcover)
978-3-7469-4088-5 (e-Book)

FSC
www.fsc.org
MIX
Papier | Fördert
gute Waldnutzung
FSC® C083411

Zeitfracht Medien GmbH
Ferdinand-Jühlke-Straße 7
99095 Erfurt, Deutschland
produktsicherheit@kolibri360.de